Crossing Frontiers

Papers in
American and Canadian
Western Literature

Crossing Frontiers

Papers in
American and Canadian
Western Literature

Edited by Dick Harrison

The University of Alberta Press 1979

First published by
The University of Alberta Press
Edmonton, Alberta, Canada
1979

Canadian Cataloguing in Publication Data

Main entry under title:
Crossing frontiers

Papers given at a conference held in Banff, Alta.,
April 1978.
ISBN 0-88864-058-7

1. Literature, Comparative—Canadian and American—
Congresses. 2. Literature, Comparative—American
and Canadian—Congresses. 3. The West in literature
—Congresses.
I. Harrison, Dick, 1937-
PS8097.A4C76   C810'.9'32   C78-002162-2
PR9185.3.C76

Book design by Christopher Ozubko

Printed by Hignell Printing Ltd.
Winnipeg, Manitoba, Canada

Contents

Acknowledgements

The Conference for which these papers were originally prepared was sponsored by the Department of English of the University of Alberta with the co-operation of the Department of History of Idaho State University at Pocatello. It was also supported by the University of Alberta; the National Endowment for the Humanities; the Canada Council; the Minister of Culture, Province of Alberta; the United States Embassy, Ottawa; and the Alumni Association of the University of Alberta. Their interest in and support of both the Conference and this volume are gratefully acknowledged.

Appreciation is also expressed to Mrs. James Thurber for permission to reprint material from her husband's work *Wild Bird Hickock and His Friends*, on pages 123-125 [Copr.©1937 James Thurber. Copr. © 1965 Helen W. Thurber and Rosemary Thurber Sauers. From *Let Your Mind Alone*, published by Harper and Row. Originally printed in *The New Yorker*] ; and to the Turnstone Press, Winnipeg, for permission to reprint material from Robert Kroetsch's *Seed Catalogue*, on pages 119, 128, and 129.

Introduction

Dick Harrison

This volume is in part a record of the proceedings of a conference held in Banff in April of 1978. It is also designed to be an autonomous book with its own coherence and completeness for readers who did not attend the conference, a book which may be a useful starting point for the comparative study of Canadian and American Western literature.

"Crossing Frontiers" brought together a selection of the most prominent historians, literary scholars, novelists and poets of the two Wests for the purpose of comparing their literatures and current approaches to them. The four-day program was built around the six major papers published here, which were written with the aims of the conference in mind. Discussion of each paper was led by a respondent who, whenever possible, had studied a draft of the paper to be delivered. In view of the undeveloped state of comparative study and the absence of authorities well versed in both fields, discussion became an especially vital part of the program. Particularly valuable in bringing out the contributions of the delegates were the series of ten panel discussions on the topics of "Comparing Frontiers in History," "Freedom and Order on the Frontier," "Woman in Western Literature," "Western Poetry," "Relationships with Minority Literature," "Historical and Mythic Wests," "Man in his Natural Environment," "Native People in Western Literature," "Popular Literature of the West" and "Literature and Film in the West," and the plenary panel session on publishing in the West. Interspersed with the papers and panels were readings by novelists and poets which added an immediate and concrete experience of the literature being compared. Most Canadian delegates had their first opportunity to hear readings by American novelists Wallace Stegner, Frank Waters and Frederick Manfred, and poets William Stafford and Keith Wilson. American delegates also expressed their sense of discovery at hearing Canadian novelists W. O. Mitchell, Rudy Wiebe and Jack Hodgins, and poets Dorothy Livesay and Andrew Suknaski. The program closed with a plenary panel session in which literary scholars and historians from each West assessed what had been accomplished during the conference.

The root idea of "Crossing Frontiers" provoked an unexpectedly strong response, not only in the number of people who came but in the depth of their involvement. Instead of the 150 expected, 280 came, including fifty Americans from as far away as Boston and Anchorage. Most considered the conference unusually rewarding. As Howard Lamar put it, "Crossing Frontiers has been one of the most important trips for the mind I have ever experienced ." The freedom of discussion and spirit of genuine inquiry which so enhanced the meetings may have owed much to the fact that such a diverse group of people were moving out of accustomed territory and approaching various geographical, disciplinary, and psychic "frontiers" in a spirit of unabashed curiosity. The range of approachable frontiers also seemed indefinitely extensible as the conference progressed. One of the most startling cultural highlights of the program was a brilliant combination of poetry reading and country-rock music created by Saskatchewan writer Ken Mitchell and a group called the Dumptrucks (Michael Taylor and Michael Millar) after the banquet. The activities became, as Henry Kreisel says in his summing up, a kind of celebration of the richness of western experience.

It would be difficult, if not unwise, to recreate in print the spirit which possessed the conference in Banff. After the celebration, what remains is the solid and accessible core of the dialogue. As the program in Appendix B will testify, it would be impossible, in a volume of any reasonable size, to do justice to the very considerable contributions of the chairmen of sessions and of the panelists and delegates in the smaller discussion groups. There are similar practical obstacles to reproducing the readings of novelists and poets. We have brought together the major papers by Don Walker, Howard Lamar, L. G. Thomas, Leslie Fiedler, Robert Kroetsch and Eli Mandel. Following each paper, with one exception, is the written response to it, providing some sense of the open dialogue in which the papers were set. The summary conclusions by Max Westbrook, Rosemary Sullivan, Henry Kreisel and Richard Etulian might be thought of as voicing the experience of the delegates at large. They express informed views of what happened at "Crossing Frontiers" as well as what might have been done and what should now be done in the study of the two literatures as a result of the conference.

As an expedition into a relatively uncharted area, the conference naturally discovered more questions than answers, but the kinds of questions raised may point to where some of the answers are buried. The paths of exploration took some unexpected turns. The first stated objective of the conference, for example, was to determine whether "two outwardly similar regions have inspired literatures which differ in their typical themes, forms and techniques," and whether differences "reflect historical and cultural differences between the regions." Yet the first impression to be gathered from the papers is of cultural similarities. Leslie Fiedler advances a continental mythology of the frontier; Eli Mandel recalls the pervasiveness of American popular culture in his Saskatchewan childhood; Robert Kroetsch traces a similar failure of sexuality in prairie fiction from Willa Cather to Sinclair Ross; Howard Lamar and Lewis G. Thomas both emphasize the persistence of settled social structure in the supposed freedom of the West; and Don Walker seeks to define a common ground between history and fiction which would have no national boundaries.

The question arises whether the similarities speak of a belief in one homogeneous West or merely common preoccupations among scholars on both sides of the border. One common concern can be seen to underlie most of these similarities. In the papers of historians and literary critics alike, the idea of myth (or legend, or stereotype) recurs in a continual series of oppositions with such terms as "history," "fact," "reality" or "authentic experience." One of the unexpected "frontiers" evoked by the conference title appears to be not national or disciplinary but epistemological, between various ways of knowing the West. The relative claims of imaginative and factual ways of knowing vary from Leslie Fiedler's description of myth as "a kind of lie which tells a kind of truth unavailable to science" to L. G. Thomas's reference to popular stereotypes which dim the realities of the Canadian past and blur the outlines of Canadian and western identities. There is a predictable difference of values here between the literary critic and the historian; what is remarkable is their common concern with contending modes of understanding. Don Walker's opening paper, "On the Supposed Frontier between History and Fiction," addresses this question most directly. Walker insists that the historian, to reach any significant truth about human experience, must go beyond the "scientific" and quantifiable. He must exercise all of the human mentality including imagination, and in this respect he engages in a creative act closely analogous to that of the fiction writer. The historian's general reliance on "fictions" large and small was referred to elsewhere in the conference, including in the panel on "Historical and Mythic Wests" where historian Douglas Owram spoke of the differing "myths" which have occupied western Canadian novelists and historians over the past half-century.

From the common preoccupations of the scholars, important similarities between the Wests do emerge. To consider first the historians, both Howard Lamar in his "The Unsettling of the American West: The Mobility of Defeat" and Lewis G. Thomas in "Prairie Settlement: Social Structures in a Canadian Hinterland" work to root out certain entrenched stereotypes of the Wests: Lamar opposes the belief that the westering impulse in America was fuelled by the lure of untrammelled freedom; Thomas discredits the popular conception of Western Canadian development as "wholly the work of the sturdy homesteaders, drawn from the ranks of the needy and oppressed of the world, who created, by heroic toil and suffering, an egalitarian, classless and unstructured society." Both argue that the social, economic and political influence of the metropolitan centres of the nations were much stronger on the frontiers than is generally assumed. Throughout the conference, in fact, historians from both nations maintained a mildly anti-Turnerian tone, questioning at least the common conceptions of the frontier inspired by Turner's work. Turrentine Jackson, in the panel on "Frontiers in History," went so far as to suggest that it is time students of comparative frontiers set aside not only Turner but all such theories and approached particular cross-border comparisons with open minds.

Amid these common concerns it should not be forgotten that the western stereotype which Thomas seeks to dispel is different from that of the American West, and so is the conception of the Canadian West he advances: a colonial society whose development and values were closely directed by an elite in central Canada. It is regrettable that Canadian historian Carl Berger was prevented by illness from attending the conference and responding to Thomas's paper, because the position Thomas adopts is in many respects controversial. While describing the prairie provinces' colonial subjection to central Canada, for example, he refrains from adopting that partisan tone which alone would satisfy most westerners. He further affronts their egalitarian sentiments by dismissing the favoured stereotype on the grounds that "it ignores the social objectives of the national government as completely as it does the attitudes of the creative minority who acted as that government's effective arm." As he says subsequently, "The very suggestion that some settlers in the west had privileges, privileges which proved an advantage rather than a handicap in making their adjustment to the western environment, provokes a hostile response on the assumption that such an assertion implies a defence of privilege by its beneficiaries."

A western regionalist might, at this point, ask whether the privileged settler should be seen as creative or as a sinister instrument of the central government in shaping a society inadequately sensitive to local needs and conditions. That is, did he make an adjustment to the western environment or merely prosper within an overall failure to adjust? Some would argue that the resultant social, economic and political structures were legacies the prairie provinces are yet struggling to recover from. If the privileges were, in fact, an advantage to individual adjustment, was the elite Anglo immigrant's rate of success higher than that of others such as the middle-European of peasant ancestry? We do know that by 1925 there were as many English immigrants returning to the old country as arriving on the prairies. Thomas's more extensive work on the subject, now in preparation, will undoubtedly provide answers for these questions and may effect a major shift in the balance of western historiography.

The familiar historical and cultural distinctions between the two Wests were more extensively outlined in the smaller discussions, particulary in the three brilliant panels on "Frontiers in History" (John Foster, Allan Smith, Turrentine Jackson), "Historical and Mythic Wests" (Brian Dippie, Kent Steckmesser, Douglas Owram), and "Law and Order on the Frontier" (James Folsom, R. C. McLeod, Michael Peterman). They grow, in large measure, out of the difference between a revolutionary nation created by a declaration of independence based on man's inalienable right to life, liberty and the pursuit of happiness, and an anti-revolutionary nation created by an act of the British parliament based on the ideals of peace, order and good government. The differences between a culture with democratic, egalitarian and individualistic ideals and one which is relatively conservative and hierarchical would obviously have their effect. Most important, perhaps, have been the differences in the way the metropolitan centres have regarded their respective Wests. The American West enjoyed a degree of autonomy and suffered a degree of disorder not tolerated in the Canadian West, which was developed as a series of orderly colonies where social institutions were commonly installed in advance of settlement. A thorough and lucid account of these differences can be found in Rosemary Sullivan's excellent closing commentary. As one member of the "Frontiers in History" panel said, "Recent work begins to show similarities in such things as settlement patterns but in general the old arguments hold."

The interplay of similarities and differences during the conference had its effect in qualifying "the old arguments." The historians, perhaps because they were conscious of addressing an uninitiated audience, seemed to take particular care to refine the popular conceptions which have, in their simplicity, obscured the intricate social fabric of both Wests. Clearly when speaking to each other we can no longer stop at crude distinctions such as that between a "wild" West and an orderly West. As James Folsom pointed out, Americans have actually been cautious about liberty and much preoccupied with law. He quoted the lines from "America" which run "And crown thy soul with self-control / Thy liberty in law." Any useful distinctions will evidently have to be based on the more subtle differences in the meaning of terms like "law" and "order" in the two Wests. The question becomes: "What sort of order, embodying what complex of values?" John Foster offered a clear paradigm for the early Canadian West in the Hudson's Bay Company trading posts where the order was strictly hierarchical, modelled on that of a British ship at sea and expressing a belief in "the paramountcy of the interests of the collectivity over those of the individual." Superficially the contrast with the individualism of the American West seems stark and simple, but paradoxically, the rigid hierarchy freed the Company officers to be amazingly sensitive to individual differences. The contrast in law enforcement is equally paradoxical. The Mounted Police, with their admirable record of asserting law without violence, would at first seem to have an absolute moral advantage over the ad hoc law enforcement of the American territories. But as R. C. McLeod explained, the same police who apprehended the suspect on the prairies were often the duly constituted magistrates who tried him. The more subtle and paradoxical distinctions which develop out of the dialogue between historians may not be as easily applied, but should tell us more reliably about the backgrounds out of which the two literatures arose.

In the literary papers of Leslie Fiedler, Robert Kroetsch and Eli Mandel, the tension between mythic and historical ways of knowing loses its aspect of a hostility of contradictory views. Fiedler, in his "Canada and the Invention of the Western: A Meditation on the Other

Side of the Border," values the mythic patterns of popular literature
as maps of the unconscious psychic territory of a continent. He quotes
Thoreau's statement, "Our truest life is when we are in dreams awake."
Kroetsch, in his "Fear of Women in Prairie Fiction: An Erotics of
Space," traces specific mythic motifs in fiction to draw broader cultural
inferences about man in the space of the plains. Eli Mandel, in "The
Border League: American 'West' and Canadian 'Region'" compares
underlying national mythologies in western poetry. For these literary
critics, myth and fact reveal things about each other; the tension
between them is generative.

The similarities and differences they uncover are again paradoxical. Kroetsch's statement that in prairie literature "marriage is no
longer functional as a primary metaphor for the world as it should or
might be" at first appears to draw Fiedler's western myth of male
bonding across the border, yet on closer inspection it appears that the
characters Kroetsch describes do not flee to the wilderness but forever
approach the desired female in love and fear. Mandel also begins in
similarities and ends in distinctions.

In his close comparison of Sinclair Ross's *As For Me and
My House* and Willa Cather's *My Antonia*, Kroetsch has opened an
extremely valuable access into the centre of these comparative studies.
He is comparing prominent literary works in their most intimate and
characteristic features of narrative structure, form and typical imagery.
Such comparisons are as yet rare and difficult to establish, by virtue
of the very disparate forms of the typical works of the two Wests.
How, for example, would one compare *As For Me and My House* with
The Oxbow Incident or *The Big Sky*?

Kroetsch's choice of parallel Edenic motifs leads to some
unexpected insights, but it also raises some questions in addition to
those found in Sandra Djwa's brilliantly incisive response to the paper.
While Edenic motifs can be found in both, man's general relation to
the natural environment in the two novels is very different. It is
not merely that the landscape in *My Antonia* is more consistently
beneficent and nurturing; man's relationship to it is also more stable.
Cather's tone usually corresponds to what David Carpenter, in the
"Man in His Natural Environment" panel, termed "geopiety," which
like any sort of piety tends to be static. Man's relationship to nature in
As For Me and My House, on the other hand, is not only painful and
precarious, it is shifting and problematic, a source and image for the
greatest emotional and spiritual struggles in the novel. This difference
may affect the way in which garden motifs can be interpreted. It may

also, as Carpenter suggested, define one of the central differences in the dramatic structure of Canadian and American western literature.

Eli Mandel, in describing his Saskatchewan childhood of playing Hollywood cowboys and unconsciously accepting baseball as his "national" sport, acknowledges the depth and complexity of our common plains heritage. In his usual uncanny way, he also arrives at that distinction between the imaginative space of the two Wests which happens to be most consistently reflected in the papers of this conference. The alternatives in Mandel's title, "West" and "Region," beget a series of related distinctions: space and border, movement across and search within, spiritual journey and search for ancestral roots, mobility and stasis. The distinctions he takes to be national rather than merely western. He quotes from Olson's *Call Me Ishmael*: "I take SPACE to be the central fact to man born in America . . . . Some men ride on such space, others have to fasten themselves like a tent stake to survive." With considerably more subtlety than this brief introduction allows, Mandel distinguishes in the poetry of Ed Dorn, Michael Ondaatje and Robert Kroetsch the American western myth of spiritual journeying through space from the developing Canadian western mythology of seeking ancestral roots within a bordered region. Two responses to space: "Some dug in. Some mounted." Mandel concludes: "If Olson is right and Space is the central fact to man born in America, Kroetsch is right to locate the central concern born to a man in Canada to be the regional myth of origins."

Mandel's conclusion has rich implications beyond the contemporary poetry he examines. In Canadian prairie fiction the journey and the identification of physical movement with spiritual change have very little prominence. Consider two classics which are sometimes compared: Twain's *Huckleberry Finn* and W. O. Mitchell's *Who Has Seen the Wind*. Huck's spiritual journey through space appears to have a function analogous to Brian O'Connal's static search for his proper relationship to the place he is in. Mandel's conclusion also illuminates certain patterns in the major papers of the conference.

Don Walker chooses to base his study on the cowboy, a central protagonist in literature of the American West. The cowboy, like the lawman, the gunfighter and the mountain man, is practically defined by his mobility. No such figure has enjoyed a comparable prominence in Canadian fiction, where the cowboy is reduced to "a hired hand on horseback," and the saddle horse itself plays only an occasional role.

The contrast between the themes of Lamar and Thomas invites similar speculations. Howard Lamar's subject is mobility, L. G. Thomas's is stasis: a process of prairie settlement carefully engineered so that westward movement would effect as little social, political and spiritual transformation as possible. Similarly, Fiedler's myth of the West is about escape, while Kroetsch's hero, even when mounted, rides around and around the house which contains the elements of domesticity and stability. The question is hard to escape. Was this combination of papers quite fortuitous or does it reflect something in the cultures of the two Wests which corroborates Mandel's conclusion?

If "Crossing Frontiers" has raised enough of such questions, it has served its purpose as an opening gambit in a dialogue between the Wests which could be long and rewarding. Many have expressed their eagerness to take part in another crossing of frontiers, but the need for further exchange is probably not as pressing as the need for basic study and research into the questions already raised. Richard Etulian, in his closing commentary, provides a detailed and systematic account of the work which should ideally lead up to a second comparative conference if we are to be sure we will not merely repeat but advance beyond "Crossing Frontiers." We hope that the present volume will stimulate some of that basic research and publication.

On the Supposed Frontier Between History and Fiction

Don D. Walker

The phrase *on the supposed frontier* has the advantage of signifying both topic and position. It indicates a discussion *of* the supposed frontier, and it locates that discussion *on* that supposed frontier. Both topic and location are of course metaphorical. Knowing the world of the historian and knowing the world of the novelist, we suppose that however much these worlds share in humanistic content and method they are nevertheless separate and that between them exists a boundary or, more likely, an area of unmarked, perhaps unexplored terrain. Both boundary and unsettled region may of course be called frontiers, but it is the latter I am supposing to exist between history and fiction, at least between western history and western fiction. The histories of western history and western fiction I believe warrant this sense of their relationship. To make the metaphor more concrete, they suggest a stretch of desert or reach of mountains yet unclaimed or, if claimed, held in dispute. Frontiers may of course be friendly places where two worlds face each other and touch in mutual consent, but they may also be settings of contention. If we assume, as we easily assume, an adversary relationship between history and fiction, we may even suppose the frontier to be a buffer zone protecting history from fiction, fiction from history. Scholars need not be diplomats; indeed like Vance Palmer they may find comfort in boundaries. It is the unknown that arouses them to their tasks. So if the frontier between history and fiction is truly an unexplored territory or if the map of it is perhaps badly out of date, it is time to question the old assumptions; it is time to venture on to that frontier. We can then hope, if historians and novelists are finally found separated, that the line of separation will prove to be a rigorously considered philosophical or methodological boundary and not merely an archaic mete of intellectual tradition.

To venture on to this supposed frontier will, I trust, seem less foolhardy if I mark on my map one special area where the trails remain vague, if tried at all, but where I can presume to go because over the years I have perhaps acquired some knowledge of the approaching terrain. Thus I choose what in the largest range of its written works can be called the literature of the cattle trade, that great collection of history and fiction dealing with cows, cowboys, and cattlemen. It is, to say the least, a mixed herd that results from this bibliographical roundup. To suppose a frontier may, at first glance, seem to suppose a facing relationship between worlds so far apart, so differently constituted that only the sturdy enterprise of the wandering scholar can join them in intellectual experience. Between Wayne Gard's *The Chisholm Trail*, a history, and Emerson Hough's *North of 36*, a novel, may lie a considerable distance. But between Ross Santee's *Cowboy*, a novel, and Edward Dorn's "Vaquero," a poem, may stretch the distance between Earth and Venus. What is assumed, then, is not that all history and all fiction should be considered vis-a-vis, but that some history and some fiction approach each other in material and method and that here, in this apparent converging, lies the supposed frontier. One identifies this frontier by noting, for example, the parallels and yet the distance or difference between Ernest Osgood's *The Day of the Cattleman* and Owen Wister's *The Virginian*.

There are of course many other parts of this sort of western frontier. I do not assume that I have chosen the most important stretch of it, and I certainly do not assume that I speak out of the center of Canadian historical and literary interests. In the American context, there can hardly be an area of more abiding interest. However, the ultimate justification of my choice comes not from that fact but from the hope, whatever the bit of frontier examined, of illuminating any frontier where history and fiction face each other. So if my specific materials are more American than Canadian, more cowboy-centered than settler-centered, I trust that my historiographical and literary meanings need bear no national or regional labels.

I

A venture into the supposed frontier may rightly begin with a brief survey of present historical positions. One quick glance will show that some popular writers are still perhaps more literary than historical. Whatever the historiographical evidence, they continue to impose grand traditional literary forms, exulting in undisciplined subjectivity, happy to celebrate the past rather than to understand it. Thus, as one of these historians sees "the rawhide years," the cattle drives up the long trail become a "great pageant of western romance."[1] However, such imaginative enthusiasm in the name of history, even as it seems to cross a frontier, does not of course map that frontier. It merely obscures it in nostalgic fervor. What merges here in an act of western faith is neither the history nor the fiction of our serious concern. This sort of history, if history it can be called, does not penetrate the unknown reaches of the western past. And this sort of literature, if literature it can be called, does not explore the unknown human worlds which challenge a serious western fiction.

Another quick glance may seem to find professional history and fiction happily sharing their truths in the ecumenical spirit of the new academic universalism. While some historians continue to suspect the writers of fiction, insisting, for example, that the literary image of the cow town marshals "violates reality"[2] and that if there is romance associated with cattle-trailing, it was created by "naive novelists,"[3] others are even recommending novels as historical sources. Years ago, when the new history was still relatively new, James Harvey Robinson set a national example by suggesting that "future historical writers when they come to describe our own days will be forced to assign the modern novel a high place in the hierarchy of sources."[4] From time to time a similar view has appeared, if not prevailed, in the historiography of regions. Western historians dealing with the cattle trade have occasionally offered lists of western novels as useful sources. However, the limitation, indeed the speciousness, of this apparent humanistic merger is usually revealed in the choice of novels. High, if not first on the lists, will likely be Andy Adams's *The Log of a Cowboy*; low, if not last on the lists, will likely be Wister's *The Virginian*. The historians are of course not saying by means of this ranking that *The Log* is a better novel than *The Virginian*; they simply mean that it is better history. Thus they are not recommending novels *as novels* at all. What interests them is the factual content of the novels, not their imaginative structure and style.

A further and closer look will show that recent professional historiography of the cattle trade, instead of closing the distance between history and fiction, has moved away from those features variously and pejoratively called romantic, novelistic, and literary. Described generally, the result has been to turn from the personal to the impersonal, from the concrete to the abstract. And need I say that fiction without concreteness and without person is empty indeed. Two instances will illustrate this sort of history. Skaggs's *The Cattle-Trailing*

Industry, while it gives a sketchy biographical attention to the leading trail-driving entrepreneurs, seeks to reduce economic history to a relationship, as the subtitle indicates, "Between Supply and Demand." Thus the rail-head markets do not teem with cowboy riotousness; the marshal does not confront the gunfighter. They teem "with economic activity as buyer and seller" meet "at the end of the trail. It was there," notes the historian, "that supply first confronted demand."[5]

Parenthetically one might observe that quite aside from its distance from fiction, considering it for a moment on purely historiographical grounds, such reduction to abstract economic drama may prove to be inadequate as history. To borrow a metaphor from a well-known Canadian historian, such history tends to present us with a ghostly ballet of bloodless economic categories.[6] While history need not of course be bloody, it would nevertheless seem to need the sense of blood moving in the living tissues of historical persons. Even economic history may need that sense of person. "After all," writes Sir John Hicks, "the way the economist develops his hypothesis is by asking the question: 'What should I do if I were in that position?' It is a question that must always be qualified by adding: 'if I were that kind of person.' . . . It is only by getting a feel of what people were like that one can begin to guess."[7]

The ultimate—and one of the most recent—in historiographical abstractions is David Gallenson's equation for profitability of the long drive. In this venture in western Cliometrics, the central concern is obviously with finding empirically valid quantitative values. Thus the data accumulates to the point where, for example, the historian can assert that Q_2 (cattle reaching market) equals 0.984 Q_1 (original trail herd).[8] Back of this equation remain of course the traditional factors, the hazards of Indians, rustlers, stampedes, and river crossings, but these are now weighted quantitatively. The first two, the historian notes, declined in importance, but stampedes and river crossings remained "quantitatively" constant and thus historiographically important.[9] In spite of high risks, in spite of the fact that a herd of 5,000 lost an average of 80 head to these assorted hazards, the rates of return were high. Needless to say, as the historian does say in his conclusion, these rates "were not realized by the drovers who were shot by irate homesteaders, scalped by Indians, trampled by stampeding cattle, or drowned while crossing flooded rivers."[10]

II
One particular phrase here provides the necessarily limited focus for
an exploration of that supposed frontier between history and fiction.
If it indicates nothing of Cliometric importance, perhaps it nevertheless
holds something of historical value. And certainly, as we shall see, it
marks a human moment over which the literary imagination has often
lingered.

      The phrase is *trampled by stampeding cattle*, and I choose it
among the others not because it pushes into our attention fraught with
significance—shooting and scalping may seem more traditionally
exciting—but because it challenges us with appropriate questions.
Reduced to its simplest terms, the historical event indicated by the
phrase offers us little more than a dead cowboy, probably nameless,
and a small group of living cowboys, also probably nameless, obligated
by circumstance to bury their dead.

      What if anything should the historian do with this event? What
if anything can he do with it? The documented instances of cowboy
death by trampling are statistically unimpressive. Thus if we insist
on number and number, we had better turn to other matters, say
to counting cows or acres or miles of barbed wire. An enterprising
Cliometrician could probably work out an equation for death on the
trail, but of what use would his equation be? Say 30,000 cowboys and
fifty dead by trampling. Cowboys reaching Abilene equals .998 times
cowboys leaving Texas. Furthermore, it seems doubtful that any death
or any sum of deaths contributed to changes, even minor, in trail
routes or herding techniques or overall operating costs for the driving
contractor. So how did it concern history that a cowboy was trampled?
The death of Jedediah Smith at the hands of the Comanches in 1831
may not have further altered history, but at least we can say that here
was a man who had mattered, his end being, as the philosopher of
history might say, a significant terminating motif in the story of
western exploration.

      Thus some will say, let us leave all trampled cowboys to folk
song and sentimental fiction. Let us remember if we must poor Charlie,
so mangled the boys all thought him dead, poor Charlie, who would
not see his mother when the work was done that fall. Let us remember
if we must that little Texas stray, poor Wrangling Joe, found at day-
break mashed to a pulp some twenty feet below.[11] But whatever the
historical authenticity of the dead cowboys who inspired the ballads
whose sad strains are invoked here, some will say that history has
nothing to do with dead cowboys. It's fitting to shed a tear as we strum

the old guitar, but as historians, for God's sake let's not get sentimental.

Now I am not suggesting that history should become senti-mental. Sentimental history is bad history just as sentimental fiction is bad fiction. Both are motivationally superficial; both fail to do what history and fiction in their own ways ought to do, that is, bring under-standing to human existence. But I am suggesting that fear of sentiment, as a part of a larger fear of subjectivity, has sometimes turned the historian away from what I am prepared to call the historian's responsibility.

Put in its most radical form, that responsibility is to under-stand, insofar as possible, the individual cowboy in that moment of ultimate historicity, death. Such a proposition will no doubt provoke from some detractors of the cowboy the response that I have now become philosophically sentimental. In some critical circles, to attach such importance to the cowboy is to arouse a good bit of intellectual sniggering. For the cowboy, these amused dissenters will answer, cannot possibly carry all of this historical significance, however well he totes his six-guns. Yet we do not really know as a matter of historical fact that he cannot carry it. The simplicity we have habitually taken for the historical cowboy perhaps cannot carry it, but we are after all not dealing here in simplicities. Simplistic history, like sentimental history, works no better for cowboys than it does for poets and kings. Thus I am suggesting what perhaps ought to be assumed as professional horse sense, that we assume no established boundaries around the historical cowboy, that we assume instead an open frontier of humanistic know-ledge into which we can yet venture, with some risks, to be sure, as may be appropriate on any frontier, but also with the possibilities of sig-nificant discovery.

The further particular assumptions that give warrant to this venture can be briefly put:

(1) The individual is historically important. Whatever the historian's focus upon the group, the class, the cultural type, he can-not disregard the individual, the individual discovered as person, for groups in their historical concreteness are after all aggregates of persons. Obviously the historian has neither the time nor the methodological means to deal with all particular persons, but knowing and valuing even one out of a hundred or one out of a thousand adds an important dimension to historical understanding. The individual cowboy, the unique cowboy, is thus important to history first of all not because he was a cowboy but because he was a person. We can say the same thing about congressmen and kings. And if this importance seems a negative

importance, in the sense that uniqueness may seem to stand against the very way of historiography, that cannot matter. History, one hopes, must ever recognize and push against its limits.

(2) The collective *cowboys* is at best a loose term of nominalistic convenience. The discreteness of the persons it collects into a group ought therefore to retard the homogenizing habits of historians. Thus we ought to discard all of the slick, easy generalizations which bring the mind to comfort and to rest. Cowboys were freedom-loving. Cowboys were intensely loyal. Cowboys were lonely and illiterate. Most of such generalizations as they appear in history are, in my judgment, ideological or literary notions, inadequately supported as history by any sort of empirical evidence.

(3) The historical existence of the cowboy held the possibility of significant experience. Without philosophical ostentation we can project over him a proposition which an influential contemporary thinker posits of all men: the "history of the human person comes into being in the encounters which man experiences, whether with other people or with events, and in the decisions he takes in them."[12] For the cowboy I do not of course mean experiences in roping and branding cows; I do not mean experiences in shooting-up cow towns. I mean, within the special focus I have established, experiences in encountering fortuitous death, that hardest of all human facts, in a world which was, whatever its thin and transient covering of trail camp amenities and pieties, starkly alien to human concerns.

(4) The most important historical content of the cowboy was what he thought and felt, not what he wore on his head and feet, except perhaps as the hat and the boots can be taken as objectifications of his life.[13] If, as Marc Bloch said, the subject matter of history is human consciousness,[14] then we are not writing the history of the cowboy unless we are dealing with his consciousness. Some doubters at this point will ask, did he have any consciousness? At least did he have any worth taking account of? And if we turn for answers to many of the so-called classics of cattle trade historiography, we may perhaps conclude that he did not. Yet surely this inner void comes from the empty-headedness of historical method, not from the empty-headedness of the cowboy.

These propositions, it should be clear, add up to no argument for the special importance of the cowboy. They apply with equal rightness to the historical mountain man, prospector, homesteader, school teacher, cattle queen, and whore. Whatever the western area, whatever the economic activities, the critical historiographical need is to understand the historical persons who lived there.

We cannot of course deal with the trampled cowboy; he has indeed become object. But those who must find and bury him, who doing so confront in him their own finitude, are another matter. What meaning, if any, could they find in this seemingly senseless and violent event? What meaning, if any, could the historian find for them? We are now, I believe, beyond the usual borders. We are, I believe, moving in the yet unexplored country where western history has so far been reluctant to go. I submit, however, that if we can respond to these questions we can perhaps illuminate not just the existence of the cowboy but also that of all western men who pitted their possibilities against the dangers and indifference of a wilderness world.

Let us, however, back up for a moment to familiar ground, the historical moment as we find it in two well-known books, the first a standard work on the Chisholm Trail, the second an "unconventional" history of the cowboy. "There was no one," writes Wayne Gard, "to conduct funeral rites for the cowpuncher who was drowned or crushed to death. Usually the trail hands wrapped the body in a blanket and, without ceremony, laid it in a shallow grave. Heavy boulders, if any were within reach, were placed on top to keep out coyotes. Some of the graves beside the trail had crude wooden headpieces, but most of them had no marker to tell what ill-fated cowboy had reached the end of his trail on the lone prairie."[15] After a more detailed account of discovery and burial, Philip Ashton Rollins added an individualized note: "At the foot of one of the noblest peaks in the Rocky Mountains lies a grave. Its occupant died in a stampede. All that was said at the interment came out hesitantly and as follows: 'It's too bad, too bad. Tom, dig a little deeper there. Hell, boys, he was a man,' and presently, when the burial had been completed, 'Bill, we boys leave you to God and the mountain.'"[16]

As historians like to ask, was this the way it actually happened? Are we thus left with a sentimental image of death at the end of the trail on the lone prairie and with a halting passage of mountain piety? Indeed, can we really believe that Rollins heard what he here tells us as history? Or had the boys perhaps been watching a bad western movie? And yet, if this seems inadequate as history, how can we make history tell us more? In short, how can we move out further into my supposed frontier?

III

To anyone who has worked in the field of cattle trade history, the many problems in dealing with events of this kind are obvious. The business history of ranches is possible because in many instances ranch managers kept thorough, if not meticulous, business records. The social history of cattle towns is possible because with the development of towns came municipal governments and courts with their records, newspapers with their often detailed reporting, and even citizens with the time and interest to keep up the local annals. But the human history of the trail drive is another matter. Few if any drovers had the time or the interest to keep daily journals. Insofar as such sources are available, they are likely to be the tersest of notes, with little or no putting down of reflection or feeling. "Swimming Cattle is the order," one of the few participant-observers wrote on May 31, 1866. "We worked all day in the River & at dusk got the last Beefe over—& am now out of Texas— This day will long be remembered by me—There was one of our party Drowned to day (Mr Carr) & Several narrow escapes & I among the no." The entry for the following day opens with mention of a stampede "last night" and closes, "Many Men in trouble. Horses all give out & Men refused to do anything."[17] It is perhaps as close as the sources will take us directly. Yet it is only one source, and we must be careful about making it typical.

The richest storehouse of historical information has been *The Trail Drivers of Texas*, a hefty compilation of more than three hundred pieces of biography and autobiography. Assuming the accuracy of some of these memories, we can perhaps reconstruct the outer movements of certain inner events, for example, the finding of a dead cowboy, his burial in his own blanket in a grave scratched out of the plains earth with axe and shovel. But beyond such simple historical configurations we cannot easily move with confidence. The soft aura of old dreams floats easily in the factual text.[18] This sort of trail history rarely if ever buries its cowboys on the open plains; it buries them on the prairie, more exactly on the lone prairie. Furthermore, it buries them where the wild roses bloom. As one trail driver remembered, "Some few [cowboys] never came back, but were buried along the lonely trail among the wild roses, wrapped in their bed blankets; no human being living near, just the coyote roaming there."[19]

Thus what purports to be a history of the trail and ranch life is often a selective, nostalgic memory. "We have forgotten the hardships and remember only the pleasant things," said one trail driver.[20] "It seems now as though it was in some other world and under fairer skies," said another.[21] Granted that history cannot be written free of present perceptions and meanings, it remains true nevertheless that even the most idealistic of histories must seek vigorously to probe back through the obscuring fogs of regionalistic sentiments and pieties, back through the drifting shadows of lore and legend. When we ask as historians, what was the meaning of death beneath the hoofs of stampeding cattle?, when we try as historians to understand that cowboy moment of shock or grief or anger, can we find answers in the comfortable pieties of nostalgic old men? "Looking back," wrote one of them, "it seems that Providential guidance has been instrumental in my living through the many harrowing experiences of the early days."[22] Did the cowboy thus feel the voice of God even in the thunder of cattle? Perhaps he did, but we must in effect ask him if we are truly to know. Teddy Blue, who also pointed them north, remembered a quite different sort of conviction: "You could pray all you damn pleased, but it wouldn't get you water where there wasn't water. Talk about trusting in Providence, hell, if I'd trusted in Providence, I'd have starved to death."[23] May it perhaps be true that the impieties of youth sometimes become the pieties of old age?

If, then, the historian has relatively few sources, if these sources are often sketchy at best, having almost no concrete immediacy, and most important if they give him only the outer shell of the event and the men involved, can history push on into the yet unknown? My answer is that it can, that it has not yet reached whatever absolute boundaries the divine map of history may have marked out for man.

We must begin our venture not with the hope of discovering rich deposits of new source material, but with the conviction that the old sources can perhaps tell us more than we have so far allowed them to tell us. New documents will undoubtedly be turned up along with the old spurs, rotted saddles, and other artifacts of the cowboy past, but these sources are likely to seem as apparently unyielding as those we already know. Thus our conviction must be based on the possibility of new ways of historical understanding. And these ways must involve what for some historians may seem radical changes in the traditional relationship between the historian and his evidence. Indeed these ways may seem to involve radical redefinitions of both *historian* and *historical evidence*. I say *may seem to*, believing that modern historiography has long sanctioned these ways, that what is new, and perhaps radical, is only their application to the historiography of the West.

The new relationship means that the historian cannot wait like a blank roll of tape for his supposed facts to speak. To learn what they mean, to give them the coherence they may at first seem to lack, he must do more than record human events; he must in a sense participate in them. He must come to his task with a capacity of empathy, re-creating, and indeed re-living. If the old empiricists, who still ride firm in the saddle, object, let us say at once that we are not thus abandoning history to the vagaries of subjectivity and idealism. To say that the historian is not subject is of course to utter nonsense; to suppose that being subject he must corrupt and distort all that he knows is to reveal a naive kind of cynicism. To argue that history must be wholly free of idealism is to favor the impossible; to suppose that such idealism necessarily means the imposition of unhistorical innate ideas upon the pure objectivity of history is to reduce history and the historian to caricature. Surely we have reached a point in the epistemology of western history where we can recognize that the historian understands by means of structures he bears within himself but that these structures may themselves nevertheless be historical in the sense that they too have been established by experience.

Thus, to understand that historical moment out of the past, we start with whatever facts and artifacts scholarly enterprise and good fortune may have provided us. We fasten ourselves if you will to whatever is given. But then we let our perceptions make their own inquiry. We let our imaginations hover over that moment, exploring relationships, critically trying out possible patterns, not with the intention of making something up but with the hope of understanding what in an important way is already there. That these imagined patterns or configurations are nevertheless similar to fictions should be obvious, and thus we may seem to have reached our boundary line, if indeed we have not already crossed it.

Such historical ventures into new territory or such new historical ventures into old territory are clearly fraught with risks. Any well-trained graduate student can perhaps write the sort of history which consists in heaping up and arranging notes gathered from a multitude of sources, but only a sensitive, disciplined, and responsible humanist can presume to give himself to the further task of understanding what those sources mean, to trusting his perceptions as well as his acquired habits of historical method. To abandon what Robert Lifton calls "exaggerated concerns with detached objectivity"[24] may not be easy, for there is comfort and safety in impersonal objectivity, even when there may not be understanding. To venture without the usual trappings may seem risky and very lonely. The bibliography may shrink; the footnotes may grow fewer and fewer. Imagine the terror in looking down a page of historical assertions and not being able to find security in the thick supporting layers of documentation.

While yet on the historical side of our supposed frontier, let us then have one further look at the cowboy in the particular trail situation upon which I have chosen to focus. Our bibliography has diminished to a single title, and a lonely footnote will account for all citations. A cowboy named Davis has been "killed," as our informant puts it, "deader than hell." "Our outfit laid off that afternoon to rest the herd and help bury him, and I remember after we got the grave dug one of the fellows said: 'Somebody ought to say something. Don't nobody know the Lord's Prayer?' I said: 'I do' So they asked me to say it over him, but I only got as far as 'Thy will be done.' and got to thinking about my brother and had to quit. You know why. I was kind of rattled anyhow."[25]

We cannot corroborate this account from other sources, but we can give it historical credence. And even more important we can find meaning in it in the sense that all of its parts can be seen to cohere into an understandable human whole. First of all it has the advantage of coming within the context of an extended autobiography. Although we may perhaps not believe every autobiographical assertion, we are nevertheless persuaded by this self-history as a whole. It suits our perception of an authentic person. Thus when that authentic person participates in the trail moment, the actions, the hints of inner response seem authentic, and not just the unmotivated gestures granted to stock figures in fragments of official memory. It is not perhaps much that we understand here. Certainly we must wish for a richer sense of this moment. And yet what we do learn is important. For the historical "I" is no longer merely a dumb object, a mute "him" who might as well be an "it" for all we know of his nature as man. It is not a full burst of consciousness, yet slight as it seems the association of this new death with the death of a brother is a kind of inner meaning, truer, one believes, than the conventional pieties with which the past is so often garnished. Truer, we should add, not just to the way a cowboy was, but truer too to the way man is. Indeed, we understand this cowboy in the past precisely because we identify with him as we claim his identity in us. To deny the use of such anthropological transferences in history would be to reduce history to the story of unknowable strangers, to leave historical cowboys as little more than quaint objects preserved in the museums of time.

If we seem now even closer to the ways of fiction, that closeness is fitting. For it is time to see the lay of the frontier from the other side.

IV

Anyone even casually acquainted with the literature of the West will remember many novels dealing with the epic drive of cattle from Mexico and Texas to the northern markets and ranges. From *The Log of a Cowboy* to the latest variation on an old theme and structure, the march of trail drive fiction goes on, apparently without end. If the last cow has been driven, the last novel is yet to be written. No one, so far as I know, has attempted an accurate tally of these books. In my personal library there are at least a dozen. In a variety of modes, at differing levels of artistic sophistication, these works delineate the experience of moving great herds of longhorns up the ladder of rivers, through dust, Indians, storms, stampedes, and the civilized violence of cow towns.

It is not, however, in one of these novels that I propose advancing upon the supposed frontier. Some of them perhaps might serve us well in this study, but if we are again dealing with a single trail situation, we can, I believe, rightly find our appropriate texts in the briefest forms, in the short story and in the short play.

When J. Frank Dobie included "Longrope's Last Guard" in his book *The Longhorns*, he called Charles M. Russell's story "perhaps the finest . . . that has ever been written about cows or cowboys."[26] Fifty miles south of Dodge City, in the worst stampede the narrator has ever seen, Longrope, a trail driving cowboy, is trampled to death. Alerted by the shots of discovery, the trail men gather and are moved to silence by what they see. The narrator observes, "Let death visit camp an' it puts 'em thinkin' . . . . He's never welcome, but you've got to respect him." Some of the men are for taking Longrope to Dodge and getting a box made for him, but a cowboy called Old Spanish says: "Boys, Longrope is a prairie man, an' if she was a little rough at times, she's been a good foster mother. She cared for him while he's awake; let her nurse him in his sleep." So wrapped in his blankets, Longrope is put to bed. And what remains to be said in the story is a sort of epilogue: after twenty years the end-gate marker has disappeared; the burial spot has returned to grass. "It sounds lonesome," the story concludes, "but he ain't alone, 'cause these old prairies has cradled many of his kind in their long sleep."[27]

It is not difficult to understand why Dobie valued this story so highly. It shows a writer with an ear tuned to authentic western speech, an eye sharp for the authentic details of men and cattle, and a heart warm to Dobie's own brand of western mysticism. In my judgment, however, it does not as fiction take us where we need to go. At the point of deepest imaginative concern, it falls into a reverential literary hush; it withdraws from concreteness and turns to the abstractness of standard, if not sentimental, personifications. If death does indeed put men thinking, what do they think? As one interested reader, I refuse to believe that they think simply that death is to be respected, that the prairie has been a good mother, that there is a kind of earthly brotherhood in her caring soil. Fiction, I believe, can do better than this—if the writer will but use it with more seriousness and sophistication.

To do better, fiction must advance into our supposed frontier. And here there are no established obstacles and limits, no academic guidebooks, no walls of high tradition. If in the judgment of some critics there seems to be presumption in the historian's effort to answer our question, there can be no question of presumption if the effort comes within the art of fiction. For pushing on toward the limits of imaginative perception, even at the risk of wandering in a mapless inner world, is to show fiction's own proper boldness. Technical problems may slow the venture, timid imaginations may choose to turn back, but final boundaries, if indeed there are any, are themselves yet to be discovered.

A second work in another form may give us better, at least different answers. Late in 1923 the Pioneer Players of Melbourne produced Louis Esson's one-act play "The Drovers." Written in a Bloomsbury flat, half a world away from the author's remembered Queensland, the play sought to evoke a sense of vast arid plains and dramatically to define the tragic predicament of a man trapped there.[28] On the long drive across the Barklay Tableland, the thirsty cattle have rushed in stampede. Briglow Bill, one of the drovers, has been badly trampled. He knows himself he's done.[29] There is nothing to do but leave him with a strong shot of pain-killer and get the mob going. As the boss says, "How in Hell can we travel with an injured man?" Thus Briglow dies, his passing sung in the sympathetic pidgeon chatter of a watching black boy.

What is the meaning of this western death? Briglow has made no tragic mistake. The jackeroo, the greenhorn, who has shot at a dingo, tries to claim responsibility, but as the boss says, "It's all a damned accident." To Briglow it doesn't matter. He says, "It had to come sooner or later. I've lived my life, careless and free, looking after my work when I was at it, and splashing my cheque up like a good one when I struck civilization. I've lived hard, droving and horse-breaking, station work, and overlanding, the hard life of the bush, but there's nothing better, and death's come quick, before I'm played out—it's the way I wanted."[30]

As an eloquent bit of bush stoicism, it will perhaps do. A man lives the good hard life; death comes before he is weak and whimpering. Maybe, as Briglow muses, the bush'll miss him a bit, the tracks he's traveled, a star or two, and the old mulga.[31] But it is a hope, not a conviction. He knows as well as those who leave him that the dry plains do not care, that, as an American cowboy might well have put it, they do not give a good goddamn whether he lives or dies.

It is simple, stark and simple, as understated as anything in the theatre of its time. Compared to the American cowboy melodrama of the same period, it is strangely underwritten. Little happens on stage; gunsmoke does not fill the air; human voices quietly sound against the vast silence of the empty plain. Perhaps the short play could say no more.

It is not, however, as deeply into the matter as I believe the imagination can go. However eloquent the drover's stoicism, it does not speak ultimate and universal answers to the question of death. The great anxiety is not so easily reckoned with. A heroic fatalism requires that man accept the fates, but is it not yet more manly to tell the fates to go to hell, to define oneself in one last gesture of rebellion against the indifferent world? There are, to be sure, no possibilities that will change the final fact of death; indeed death is the most certain of all human possibilities. However, that certainty need not mean that man merely lives to die; on the contrary, it can mean that even in dying man lives.

If we seem to have moved away from the cowboy and drover, it is only the traditional versions of these fictive persons that we have left behind. I grant that the standard cowboy of most Westerns cannot hold the sorts of meanings I am suggesting. However, I believe this incapacity reveals not so much the inherent weaknesses of the fictive cowboy as the imaginative weaknesses of the western writer. I have mentioned technical problems. There is, for instance, the matter of point of view. As long as we seem stuck with a choice between innocent Eastern greenhorns and quaint old-timers whose brains and nerves are made of boot leather, we haven't, I'm afraid, much hope of moving on. The innocent has been a sensitive instrument with which freshly to see the ranges, deserts, and mountains, and of course from Mark Twain to the present we have used him for initiation in the western rites of manhood. The old-timer has had his uses too. We could always look at him and see the enduring western habits of work and survival. But neither innocence nor habit is worldly and open enough to serve as the mode of consciousness. If the fictive cowboy is to represent not just the dumb kid or the brush buster who follows cows up the trail but men as they deal with their condition as man, then something much more complex, with a wider capacity of thought and feeling, must be imagined.

We left the historical frontier at the point of its concern with the way man is. I have now moved fiction to a similar concern. Has the supposed frontier thus entirely disappeared? I think not, if this disappearance means that history and fiction have merged. To be sure, they have met at a point of common humanistic interest, but their materials, their approaches, their perspectives remain nevertheless different. They meet at this common point, yet they remain apart. Using what I trust is an appropriate metaphor, I say that they remain separated by at least a single strand of fence wire. But that wire, I should add, need not be barbed.

There is finally a further way of showing this close relationship between history and fiction. "History alone," wrote an influential philosopher, "shows what man is."[32] But some will still prefer to say that history alone shows what man was, not what he is. And some will still insist that it is fiction and the other imaginative forms that show what man is. In the classic distinction, history tells what happened, poetry tells what happens. History deals in the unique, poetry in the universal. Thus to say that history shows what man is is somehow to speak unhistorically just as to say that fiction (substituting that term for poetry) shows that man is historical is somehow to speak unpoetically. However, the apparent difficulty is resolved if we explicate the quoted proposition by a brief extension: history shows what man is, and what man is is historical. To use a less ambiguous term, man in his very nature possesses historicity. This means that man is historical not because he stands in history, surrounded and swept willy-nilly by the passage of time, but because he is temporal in the very basis of his being.[33] The study of man's past shows this anthropological truth; the imaginative study of his present and his future shows it too. Historical researches lead to this insight; imaginative studies of existence confirm it.

Thus, while there may be petty quarrels and active skirmishes, there need be no field of bloody contention between history and fiction. If the historian observes that a fictional cowboy violates history because he (the cowboy) wears an unauthentic pair of pants, he (the historian) may be right, right, that is, about the pants. However, such observation has really nothing whatsoever to do with the cowboy's existence in history. And if the novelist claims he is being properly historical by documenting his setting as the original Abilene or Tombstone or Los Angeles, he may be right too, right, that is, about the accuracy of his setting. However, such documentation has really nothing whatsoever to do with a character's historical existence. The claims and counter-claims, the storing up of extraneous facts like ammunition, the manning of forts of disciplines in academe are thus so much thrashing about beside the important point, so much show obscuring what truly matters. Facing each other across that barbless wire, the historian and the novelist, one comes to believe, have finally nothing to shout or shoot about.

Notes

1   Glenn R. Vernam, *The Rawhide Years: A History of the Cattlemen and the Cattle Country* (New York: Doubleday, 1976), p. 64.

2   Robert R. Dykstra, *The Cattle Towns* (New York: Alfred A. Knopf, 1971), p. 123.

3   Jimmy M. Skaggs, *The Cattle-Trailing Industry: Between Supply and Demand, 1866-1890* (Lawrence: University Press of Kansas, 1973), p. 123.

4   James Harvey Robinson, "The Newer Ways of Historians," *American Historical Review*, 35 (1930), 255.

5   Skaggs, p. 73.

6   Frank H. Underhill, "Some Reflections on the Liberal Tradition in Canada," in *Approaches to Canadian History*, ed. Ramsay Cook, Craig Brown, and Carl Berger, intro. by Carl Berger (Toronto: University of Toronto Press, 1967), p. 41.

7   John Hicks, *A Theory of Economic History* (Oxford: Clarendon House, 1969), p. 6. G. E. Fussell has recently made a similar point in the context of farming history: "It is . . . the human person who makes changes." "Farming History and Its Framework," *Agricultural History*, 51 (1977), 138.

8   David Gallenson, "The Profitability of the Long Drive," *Agricultural History*, 51 (1977), 751.

9   Gallenson, p. 750.

10   Gallenson, p. 758.

11   For the full texts of "When the Work's All Done This Fall" and "Little Joe the Wrangler," see John A. Lomax and Alan Lomax, collectors, *Cowboy Songs and Other Frontier Ballads* (New York: Macmillan, 1938), pp. 74-76, 91-93.

12   Rudolph Bultmann, *The Presence of Eternity: History and Eschatology* (New York: Harper and Brothers, 1957), p. 43.

13   That is, outer representations of inner thoughts and feelings. A poem is clearly an objectification; however, a boot may represent nothing more than acceptance of peer practice and available product.

14   Marc Bloch, *The Historian's Craft*, intro. by Joseph R. Strayer, trans. by Peter Putnam (New York: Vintage Books, 1953), p. 151.

15   *The Chisholm Trail* (Norman: University of Oklahoma Press, 1954), p. 139.

16   Philip Ashton Rollins, *The Cowboy* (1922; rpt. New York: Ballantine Books, 1973), p. 251.

17   George C. Duffield, "Driving Cattle from Texas to Iowa, 1866," *Annals of Iowa*, XIV (April 1924), 252.

18   "I must say," noted one trail driver, "that the trail drives appear now more like a dream than a reality." *The Trail Drivers of Texas*, ed. J. Marvin Hunter (Nashville: Cokesbury Press, 1925), p. 587.

19   Hunter, p. 218.

20   Hunter, p. 768.

21   Hunter, p. 665.

22   Hunter, p. 825. See also: "A kind and all-wise Providence guarded us through all the dangers and hardships of pioneer life and will be with us to the end" (p. 766).

23   E. C. Abbott ("Teddy Blue") and Helena Huntington Smith, *We Pointed Them North, Recollections of a Cowpuncher* (Norman: University of Oklahoma Press, 1954), p. 29.

24   Robert Jay Lifton, "On Psychohistory," *Explorations in Psychohistory, The Wellfleet Papers*, ed. Robert Jay Lifton and Eric Olsen (New York: Simon and Schuster, 1974), p. 32. "Recognizing that subjective distortion can render the advantage [of beginning from concrete information that is the product of his own direct perception] a mixed one, so can it be said that exaggerated concerns with detached objectivity have too often caused us to undervalue what can be learned of history from our direct perceptions."

25   Abbott and Smith, p. 38.

26   Charles M. Russell, "Longrope's Last Guard," in *The Longhorns*, ed. J. Frank Dobie (Boston: Little, Brown, 1941), p. 130.

27   Russell, p. 138.

28   For an account of the writing of the play, see Vance Palmer, *Louis Esson and the Australian Theatre* (Melbourne: University of Melbourne Press, 1948), pp. 16-19.

29   Louis Esson, "The Drovers," *Six One-Act Plays* (Sydney: Mulga Press, 1944), p. 7.

30   Esson, p. 15.

31   Esson, p. 15.

32   *W. Dilthey, Selected Writings*, ed., trans. and intro. by H. P. Rickman (Cambridge: Cambridge University Press, 1976), p. 84. Ortega y Gasset, whose philosophy of history is germane here, called Dilthey "the most important thinker of the second half of the nineteenth century." *History as a System and Other Essays Toward a Philosophy of History* (New York: W. W. Norton, 1941), p. 216.

33   The image here comes from Heidegger. It may be useful to acknowledge this borrowing not because Heidegger was an authority on the cowboy, but because his philosophy may help us deepen our understanding of any man in history and fiction, including the cowboy. Excepting some curious allusions in Dorn's *Slinger*, Heidegger has had scant mention in western studies. Indeed, the very absence of Sartre and Heidegger may mark a sort of pre-literary stage of western settlement. One supposes, however, that historical and literary understanding of the West is not limited to indigenous intellectual resources.

Response: On the Supposed Frontier Between History and Fiction

Delbert Wylder

As a fellow humanist, I can certainly sympathize with Don Walker's concept of an unbarbed, one-stranded wire frontier between history and fiction or, more precisely, between the historian and the fiction writer. Each of these is a creator, through thought and words. As writer, each imposes some kind of order upon an external, and in some cases, an internal, universe that, without the order, would appear to the unreflective eye as chaos. Don Walker has also suggested that that single strand of fence wire is a meeting-place of common humanistic interest, and that differences still exist between "their materials, their approaches, their perspectives." But I find it difficult to think that the wire itself is not a more formidable object, one that becomes more formidable as the twentieth century nears its close. The wire seems to me to be much like Emerson's iron wire upon which the beads are strung—the iron wire of temperament. That wire becomes ever thicker, and every bead strung upon it becomes a singular barb.

What seems clear from Don's reduction on the historical frontier to that unbarbed wire is what I consider to be his belief that the present trend in history need not be toward the social sciences but should be, and hopefully will be, toward the humanistic temperament. But despite his hopes, the present trend of historians is toward the social sciences, and his own example of the economic historians is a case in point. William James saw one of the major philosophical problems as the attempt to bring into relationship two human "passions," that of feeling the need to bring the "facts of the world in their sensible diversity" into some form of simplicity, as in generalization, while at the same time feeling the necessity for distinguishing the parts rather than comprehending the whole; that is, specialization. As he suggests, "A man's philosophic attitude is determined by the balance in him of these two cravings."[1] In recent years, of course, the historian has tended toward specialization, and toward seeing human events from a perspective almost totally created by the materialistic temperament. Numbers are of utmost importance, these people would have us believe, because they can be computerized, and thus objective truth can be ascertained.

The fiction writer, on the other hand, has a dedication to the personal, toward the individual. It is true that some recent socio-logically-inspired critical theory suggests that fiction, in order to satisfy, must move from the individual to the group man, and that the tradition of the concentration of writers upon a hero or anti-hero, at least a protagonist, must be discontinued in an age in which the individual has decreased in consequence, but the fact of the matter has been that fiction, western or whatever, Canadian or American, has continued and will continue to focus its attention upon the relationship of the individual to his or her outward and inward terrain. As Don Walker has noted, "fiction without concreteness and without person is empty indeed."

An examination of one of Don Walker's statements may serve to illustrate the point. When he introduces his analysis of the phrase "trampled by stampeding cattle," he notes that in the most simple terms, we are left with one dead cowboy, plus a small group of living cowboys who are "obligated by circumstance to bury their dead." In more complex terms, however, that small group of cowboys is left with either no obligation whatever or with more than one obligation, and the obligations are based upon human value systems. There may be a moral obligation to bury the dead, but there is no *reason* for burying the lone cowboy. Perhaps the remaining cowboys will be more secure, psychologically, since they know that the group will pause to bury them if they should be tramped. But the body will decay, sooner or later, anyway, and the markers set at the head of the grave will deteriorate, too, in wind and weather. There is also a conflicting obligation to get the cattle to the marketplace, an obligation which may be more than financial, since herds often contained more than the property of one owner. If the herd has separated, it must be gathered. Stragglers must be found and returned. There is work to be done after a stampede. Even in the situation described in the quotation from Teddy Blue Abbott, that "Our outfit laid off that afternoon to rest the herd and help bury the dead cowboy," though there is present a pragmatic reason (rest the herd—and one assumes the men and the horses, too) for the delay, certain situations might have demanded that the men push on. And despite the fact that it might have been difficult to find one cowboy in the group with enough of a religious background to quote the Lord's Prayer in its entirety, each individual cowboy would have reacted differently, from different religious or moral views, from different psychological needs or fears, and different attitudes toward work, or comradeship, or financial exigencies. In fiction, of course, these conflicts between human desires, human needs, and human values are at the center of things.

From the center, a work of fiction expands outward. Through the use of characterization, tone, symbol, image, mood, the fiction writer presents parts of one fictional life in a complexity suggestive of other lives and of more elaborate meanings. The fiction writer tries to demonstrate and, in the process of demonstration, expand on meaning. The typical work of history, on the other hand, converges toward the center, for it is a work of explanation. The historian examines the data and, through a process of selection (which of course implies elimination of some data and retention of other data) and of ordering, imposes meaning or significance upon that data. His main function, it seems to me, is to provide some human "meaning" to related data, whether these data be lives or actions of political parties or government or nations or armies, or even numbers.

The fiction writer and the historian, then, would appear to have quite different approaches, and quite different temperaments. Thus, the "frontier" seems to be quite significant. The most obvious meeting ground would be, at least apparently, the historical novel, and the historical novelist would be sitting precisely on that wire that Don sees as the separation. But, an old Western saying, "The man who always straddles the fence gets a mighty sore crotch" is particularly appropriate here, and the position of the historical novelist illustrates, perhaps, how strong and thick is that fence of separation in actuality. For the historical novelist finds limited acceptance in either field. The literary critic has little consideration for the historical novel, with the exception of such works as Tolstoy's *War and Peace* which gains acceptance because it "transcends" the limitation of the genre, and the historian more often than not is disgruntled by the addition of fictional characters within the "reality" of history, and of the "distortion" and "lack of objectivity" that comes from seeing the times through the vision of that central character. To change the image, then, this unbarbed wire seems more like a vast no-man's land filled with barbed wire entanglements that allow no crossing whatever.

It will be not just interesting, but of crucial importance, to see whether or not historians move more and more toward quantification —toward what, at least superficially, appears to be a more scientific approach to the study of human existence, or whether it turns toward an avowed interpretation of that existence. In other words, it is crucial to the humanities whether or not historians consider themselves as scientists or humanists. The financial gains, of course, will be significantly greater if they choose to become "scientific," especially in the United States. It is difficult for me to believe that a conference such as this one, for example, could possibly be funded under our National Endowment for the Humanities guidelines. It does not have a social science orientation nor a concern with contemporary public policy issues. On the other hand, a return to a more "humanistic" history may well make the study of history more meaningful to the non-specialist. It may well be that, in the arts, the humanities, and even the social sciences, just as in the sciences, we have created insurmountable barriers between ourselves, and between ourselves and the populace, through our passion for specialization.

That is, however, another problem. What Don Walker seems to hope for is a better understanding of humanity from both Western fiction and Western history. He wants us to look more closely at the evidence we already have. I am reminded of Nathaniel Southgate Shaler's biography, in which he tells of his apprenticeship under Louis Aggasiz. Shaler, with all the self-confidence generated by having a new degree in hand, was asked by Agassiz to look at, not dissect, a fish. Shaler spent weeks on the task, and thought that Agassiz had forgotten him. Finally, Agassiz visited his laboratory, looked at Shaler's notes, and told him he still hadn't seem the fish. Finally, Shaler saw that he was supposed to *see*—but in a context not limited by his earlier exposure to scientific methodology. And he began to see. The Cowboy, of course, is more significant than a fish.

Perhaps this is what Don Walker suggests that we do in the study of the cowboy. We are, as historians, to cross that frontier, no matter what its size, into the area of person and mood and feel of the times. And where better to find it than in the best of fiction and the best of film? What better way to start to understand the American depression, for example, than to read novels of the depression? And not just the eastern or urban novels of Dos Passos, di Donato, Henry Roth, or James T. Farrell, but the midwestern and Western novels of Steinbeck, and Guthrie, and Manfred, particularly the latest, *Green Earth*. And it should be noted that counting the number of Englekings and Alfredsons doesn't provide much meaning. Not one character is a precisely equal one, as counter, to another one. What better way to understand the feel of the Mennonite community, including the young and rebellious ones, than from Wiebe's *The Blue Mountains of China*? And for the creative writer, the exploration of the humanistic history of any period can only give him or her a better understanding of the total context for his characters and their actions. Don Walker sees the potential in crossing frontiers, and as a fellow humanist, I will hope right along with him that the potential can and will be realized, that frontiers will be crossed more frequently than in the past and that, furthermore, we will applaud rather than denigrate those attempts to cross them. But being something of a realist, I am afraid that with the differences in approach, and in methodology, and finally in temperament, and with the twentieth century insistence on specialization, the frontier will grow wider and wider.

Note

1   William James, *The Will to Believe and Other Essays in Popular Philosophy* (New York: Dover Publicatons) pp. 65-66.

The Unsettling
of the American West:
The Mobility of Defeat

Howard R. Lamar

I must begin by paying tribute to Dick Harrison for choosing one of the most attractive, deceptive and diabolically intriguing titles for a conference that I have ever seen. The phrase "Crossing Frontiers" seemed so obvious and innocent at first. American scholars were crossing into Canada to share findings about Western literature and history. Then there was the crossing of respective disciplinary borders by historians, novelists, poets, critics, and literary scholars. But the phrase began to have so many other meanings I began to get nervous. The presence of Earl Pomeroy, whose famous essay, "Toward a Reorientation of Western History,"[1] breached a psychological barrier to new ways of approaching the American West, certainly meant that new conceptual ideas about the West were in the offing.

     A conversation with Professor Harrison did not reassure me. He said, "talk about whatever you feel is appropriate, and if you choose to throw in something about Canada that would be fine." That remark led me to a crash reading course in the history of the Prairie Provinces, which introduced me to Richard Allen's *A Region of the Mind*, an edition of excellent papers relating to Canadian Plains Studies which were presented at a conference in Banff in 1973.[2] After reading Eli Mandel's brilliant essay, "Images of Prairie Man," I concluded that Banff conferences were extremely sophisticated, subtle and psychological in approach. Those characteristics of excellence are always unnerving to a western historian.[3] I was further reduced after reading Donald Greene's splendid 1968 essay on "Western Canadian Literature," as well as his review article of Donald Davie's "Collected Poems" in the *Queen's Quarterly*,[4] in which both of them handle western and frontier themes so well. In his *Six Epistles to Eva Hesse* Davie describes in a few unforgettable lines the whole meaning of the Lewis and Clark expedition:

A breakthrough into spaciousness,
New reaches charted for the mind,
Is solid service to mankind.[5]

After that I came to attribute so many meanings to "Crossing Frontiers"
that I was reduced to an academic jelly of equivocation and indecision.
        My first response was to retreat to an actual saga of crossing
frontiers: the overland trails experience that at least four hundred
thousand Americans underwent between 1840 and 1869. Here one
could rely on a body of true folk accounts of the most traumatic
crossing of physical frontiers in the American past. Although as many
as three thousand diaries and journals may have been written about
the journey, only approximately eight hundred of those are available
today. In a forthcoming study of the overland trails, entitled *The Plains
Across*, John D. Unruh has observed "that in the entire American
experience probably only the Civil War has called forth a commensurate
cornucopia of letters, journals, diaries, memoirs, and reminiscent
accounts." They constitute, says Unruh, "a veritable folk literature
of one of the nation's greatest achievements."[6]
        It is perhaps an extraordinary tribute to the influence of
Frederick Jackson Turner and his frontier hypothesis that historians
using the many hundreds of available diaries and journals have focussed
almost exclusively on the hardships and dangers of the trail as manifested in the individual's confrontation with nature and the environment.
Such an approach completely ignores information about social institutions, family structure, the response of women, and the religious views
held by the overlanders. In short, the approach ignores their culture.
Having been sensitized to the histories of families and women, and of
race and ethnicity by my students and colleagues over the past decade,
it has been exciting to penetrate the minds of these diarists from these
new perspectives.
        So strong has the Turnerian theme of the individual *versus*
the environment been, that for many years it was assumed that once
the migrant was on the trail, he or she was outside the bounds of
society and the social contract was dissolved. In 1945, however,
David M. Potter questioned that assumption in his *Trail to California,
The Overland Journal of Vincent Geiger and Wakeman Bryarly*.[7] Potter
found that all kinds of constitutions and written rules of conduct
were drawn up by members of wagon trains. More recently Professor
John Phillip Reid has analyzed overland diaries to ferret out the
immigrant's attitude towards property. Reid's findings suggest that

the respect for property appears to have been so great among members of the wagon train that there were almost no occasions of theft or unlawful seizure. There were, in fact, so many legal arrangements about sharing goods purchased in common, and such elaborate strata-gems to dispose of common property fairly, the process became a ritual of legal moves and countermoves.[8] Undoubtedly the most extreme case of attempted division occurred on the southern trail across Arizona when one of four men, who jointly owned a wagon, decided to break away and take his share. The dissident member attempted to take a wheel and saw off a fourth of the wagon as his rightful portion. Through force and hard talking the three other men and "Dick," a slave belonging to one of the three, persuaded their ex-partner to make other arrangements. A few days later the latter tried to beat up the slave as a way of expressing his discontent. When the slave was rescued by his master he turned on his tormenter and exclaimed: "You are a nasty buzzard's puke!" Surely that must be one of the best lines recorded in an overland diary.[9]

Again one finds that the emphasis on the struggle with nature and the praise of the pioneer spirit ignores central components in a life structure—occupation, family, ethnicity, religion, peer relations and leisure—that have greatest significance for the self.[10] A close reading of two hundred overland journals strongly suggests that religious, regional and family ties and family organization were much stronger institutions than the company constitutions. The presence of families raises questions both about the prevalence of rugged individualism and the impact of the trek on families as opposed to the impact on individuals. We know that persons often left one train and joined another because the new train included citizens from their home state or county. Others sought out wagon trains whose members belonged to the same religious demonination. In addition, a large number of migrants on the central trail were devoted Sabbatarians, while others sought out prohibitionist trains or caravans in which the members had taken an oath not to swear.[11]

What emerges in the way of a group character for the migrants is that they were middle class, even Victorian in their values. With the exception of frontier Missourians and some Southern groups, even the rural frontier folk of the Middle West appear to have had Victorian values.[12] Among other things, this meant that when they encountered other groups, whether from a different region of the United States, or a different culture, they were suspicious of the strangers and often disgusted by their habits. A typical remark by an Ohio man about a

Missouri train was that they were "hogs personified." An encounter with half-breeds or Anglo-Americans who had married Mexican or Indian women, provoked the diarists, whether male or female, to express horror and disgust.[13]

At first they hated and feared Indians, an obsession not alleviated by the frequent theft of stock by Pawnees at the beginning of the trek. Further along the trail, however, they were impressed by the Sioux, Cheyenne, Cayuse and Shoshone tribes almost to the point of deciding that these savages were both noble and handsome.[14] But when Digger Indians began to raid emigrant stock on the hardest section of the California Trail, the old hatred returned with a vengeance.

An initial disgust with all Mexicans was modified by a conviction that Mexican women were beautiful, spirited, gracious and sensual. Male overlanders persuaded themselves that Mexican ladies craved off-spring from them so they could produce a stronger race than they could by mating with Mexican men.[15] However cautious most diarists were in committing very personal thoughts to the page, there is a clear sexual response to half-breeds, Indians, Mexicans and Mormons.[16] The historians of ethnicity and sexuality could have a field day with overland diaries.

In similar fashion students of women's history can find much here that is significant. It appears on reading the diaries closely, that married women with families did not want to go to Oregon or California and felt that being ripped from a family-centered world full of brothers and sisters, aunts and uncles, and cousins was cruel. Many journals suggest that a wife consented to go only if a brother and his wife went along. In some cases an extended family of twenty or more would migrate together. Put another way, the decision to go was almost always made by the men, and the women had to accept it or remain behind. If I may use the title of this paper symbolically for a moment, it was unsettling for the women—a time of dislocation and disorientation, writes Professor Lillian Schlissel—while it was adventure and opportunity for the men.[17] There is an account of a train so badly scared by an outbreak of cholera on the trail that the group turned back. The men were furious and frustrated, wrote one observer, but the women were all smiles and laughter. In another instance a wife set fire to the family wagon to protest the trip.[18]

In these examples we can see the mobility of defeat theme, for it appears that many women were persuaded that they could not have a better life in the West than they had had at home. But the record also suggests that the response of most women, once they had made the move, was to found schools, urge a move from farm to town, and to try to recapture the society they had left behind. The sense of defeat by moving was not confined to the overland trails period. Seth Humphrey in his *Following the Prairie Frontier* evokes the same theme as he witnesses a farmer and his family lined up for the Cherokee Strip run in Oklahoma in the late 1880s:

> He [the farmer] does better at wrestling with the tariff than at making a living for his wife and children. His farming is a joke. He moves further on every year—broke but with one more in the family. And he lays everything except the child to the currency. For months he has been camping all the way down from "Ioway" or some other state so that he may have, at last, a farm of his own in the Cherokee Strip. But now his cocksureness wobbles; something in the figures lined up ahead dispels his dream of a home for the asking. His great lumbering wagon cannot make the run—that much he grasps —so he proceeds to "on-hitch" his least winded plow horse and gets astride. As the Don Quixote outfit shuffles to the front, the children squall, and the chickens squawk, while his long-suffering much-better half prays tearfully that this once in their dreary lives good fortune may smile upon them.[19]

Wallace Stegner in *Wolf Willow* speaks to a larger theme of defeat when he writes of his Canadian boyhood home: "Whitemud, a generation past its pioneering stage, demonstrates all over again how much of amenity and the refined intelligence is lost when civilized men are transplanted to a wilderness. It raises the question, unthinkable to pioneers but common enough among their expatriate sons, whether any Whitemud can hope to develop to a state of civilization as high as that which some of its founders abandoned."[20]

If one tries to use new methods to understand the men on the overland trails, the factor of age appears to be a crucial one. In the thirty-year period under consideration (1840-1870) a majority of them seem to have been in their late teens or twenties. Very few of them were over forty. While the trek to the gold fields or Oregon was not a children's or youth's crusade, many did go at exactly the time they were experiencing a rite of passage to manhood. Besides the lure of gold and the desire for adventure there were many other reasons for going: the desire to escape the parental family, to get away from a dull town or an incompatible wife, or simply to shake off a sense of failure.[21]

James G. Malcolm from Batesville, Arkansas left his wife in 1849 exclaiming in his first letter to her that "if I could get one look at you before I leave I could be content; but that is impossible, thairfore I must be contented by seeing you in Emagination [sic] ." While vowing that he missed her desperately, he noted in a later letter that he was sorry she could not get enough sewing to earn an income but he urged her to keep trying. Malcolm protested for three years—until 1852—that he was coming home, but somehow he managed to go to Oregon and buy a farm there before finally returning to Arkansas.22

Captain David DeWolf of Springfield, Ohio sincerely claimed that he missed his wife saying eloquently in one of his letters: "If a man wants to learn the value of a wife let him have one and leave her and come to California; and if he does not wish himself back many times then he is far ahead of me . . . ." But DeWolf is unwilling to come home until he makes enough to get "us a home and so I can be independent of some of the damned sonabitches that felt themselves above me because I was poor. Cuss them I say and I understand they prophesy that I will never come back. Damn their stinking hides! If God spares my life I will show them to be false prophets . . . ."23

The examples are endless: John A. Johnson of Lower Sandusky, Ohio left his wife and children in 1849 to go to California for the purpose of making money and regaining his health, for he had a terrible set of lungs. Johnson was homesick the whole time he was away and his health did not improve. But despite these factors and his lack of success at mining, he wrote of moving on to Hawaii to make money by raising farm products for the California market. Eventually the real reason for his going to California was expressed in a letter to his wife when he confided to her that he hated Lower Sandusky!24 Thus DeWolf and Johnson were damned if they stayed and damned if they returned.

To reiterate a point made earlier, these and many other men, with or without families, were engaged in a physical trip west that coincided with a rite of passage to manhood. And that suggests why the frontier has had such incredibly strong masculine connotations and is associated with mastery over the environment. The point I wish to make here, however, is that the experience also often shocked or defeated the young migrant through death, disease, failure and even the decision to return. Kevin Starr in his *Americans and the California Dream*, observes that so many unanticipated troubles beset the gold seekers in California that after undergoing a modern Odyssey they underwent an Iliad as well. The gold rush experience was, in his words,

"A civil foreign war, a saga of communal ambition and collective misbehavior, a poem of expatriation, hostile gods and betrayal."[25] It was, in part, a haunting fear of failure that pushed men on to California and Oregon, and then later on to Nevada, the Fraser River, Montana, Pike's Peak, Tombstone and even the Klondike.

Two other recent studies of the gold rush also explore aspects of human defeat which historians have previously ignored. Rudolph Lapp in his *Blacks in Gold Rush California* finds that free blacks and fugitive slaves living in the New England and Mid-Atlantic states saw in golden California both new opportunities and—after 1850—a way to escape the fugitive slave law. Encouraged by Frederick Douglass, an exceptionally able and articulate group of black Americans went to California in the 1850s, "the first major voluntary migration of Afro-Americans to travel this distance for self-betterment."[26] Some achieved modest success, but they also found that the California laws were rigged against them regarding equal rights of testimony and opportunities for an equal education for their children. So frustrated were at least four hundred of the black overlanders that they accepted an invitation to come to Vancouver Island. Indeed, they called British Columbia "God's Rescue," and a black poet, Priscilla Stewart, wrote of the move:

> God bless the Queen's Majesty
> Her sceptre and her throne
> She looked on us with sympathy
> And offered us a home.
> Far better breathe Canadian air
> Where all are free and well
> Than live in slavery's atmosphere
> And wear the Chains of Hell.[27]

Professor Lapp has also found that while black Americans succeeded in finding jobs in California and were not the targets of race hatred that the Chinese, Indians and Mexicans became, mobility produced no dramatic results for them. Indeed, Lapp discovered that those from northern areas drifted to cities while those from rural southern states went to rural California.[28]

Lack of success was not confined to laborers and rural gold seekers. In *Fortunes and Failures*, a study of white collar mobility in nineteenth-century San Francisco, Peter R. Decker has tried to see if the Jeffersonian ideals of meritocracy and the gospel of the self-made man provided opportunities in the Golden Gate city for both white and blue collar workers that were not available in eastern cities.[29] Decker is particularly interested in white collar workers in San Francisco since the city was a merchant dominated town during the first three decades of its existence. Using the extensive records of the R. G. Dun Company —the nineteenth-century parent of Dun and Bradstreet—Decker found that the failure of the top echelon San Francisco merchants to maintain their status was notable, and that while petty merchants often made it to the status of general merchant, fewer blue collar workers made it to white collar status than did their counterparts in eastern cities.[30] Moreover, American-born merchants failed and fled in such large numbers that by the 1860s and 1870s the foreign-born merchants had replaced the pioneer merchants. This pattern comes as even more of a surprise when one realizes that more of the pioneer merchants were from the cities and towns of the New England and Mid-Atlantic regions than elsewhere. One is also struck by their relative youthfulness. Of the more than three thousand merchants there, 81 percent were between the ages of twenty-eight and forty.[31] In all fairness to the merchants one must add that between 1848 and 1858 they were hit by four business cycles, several major fires, and an earthquake.

Decker agrees with Richard Maxwell Brown that the frustration of failure is what made the merchants join and lead three major vigilance committees so they could eliminate the "chanciness" of the 1850s.[32] But bringing law and order to the city did not help much. By 1880 San Francisco had become a modern industrial town and the merchant class had lost its original preeminent position. Earl Pomeroy has written that "a large part of [Western] opportunity was the opportunity to imitate an older society."[33] Ironically many San Francisco merchants could not even achieve that goal. Professor Decker concludes that if both the white and blue collar workers of San Francisco had stayed in eastern cities the chances of advancement would have been better.[34]

It is startling to see how this negative side of the western saga was ignored by writers. In 1968 Robert H. Walker made a study of four hundred volumes written about the frontier by poets between 1870 and 1905. He found the poet in "approximate agreement with Turner's idea that the frontier, through initiating a series of stages in society commencing with the primitive, would encourage the purification and improvement of the American character and institutions."[35] In short, they celebrated the pioneer spirit, the trail blazer and the martyrs of the Alamo first, the growth of cities and towns and commerce and industry next, and last but not least, they praised the natural aspects of the western scene. The last topic became, in fact, the subject of one-third of all western verse written in the thirty-five year period. For the poet the West was not just a refuge but a paradise. Los Angeles was a gardener's dream, Iowa was to be a new Athens and California a new Italy. So far did the poet Wallace E. Newell take the argument in his poem, "California *versus* Heaven," that California won hands down.[36] One wonders if even Sarah Binks went that far in her praise of the Prairie Provinces.

James B. Adams echoed the sentiments of many other poets in their celebration of the city when he wrote the following about Denver in 1899:

> Love to see the stir and bustle
> In the busy town,
> Everybody got a wad a'
> Ready cash laid by.
> Aint no flies in Colorado
> Not a cussed fly.[37]

On the negative side Walker could not find a single poet who praised the Indian. And in the realm of rural and farm topics the poems sounded one consistent note: that of failure. "It is interesting to find," writes Walker, "that when the poet set out to promote his western home, whether he labored under subsidy or under inspiration, he almost never boasted of agricultural prosperity or rural felicity."[38]

The story of migration to Utah has been so dominated by Mormon historians that non-Mormon scholars have, in large part, either accepted or ignored this remarkable migration of American and European peoples to the Great Basin. Once again the stress has been on over-coming and the ultimate success the Mormons had in establishing Zion in Deseret. As Wallace Stegner says in his *The Gathering of Zion, The Story of the Mormon Trail,* "They have a stylized memory of the trail journey as a rite of passage into the kingdom." He feels that they were a "community and even a culture on the march,"[39] a point I would like to come back to later. What we tend to forget is that it was the first of the mass white refugee migrations west. It was a flight from danger and failure in Missouri and Illinois. Like Biblical tribes of old, they were fleeing persecution and, to them, an evil society. The recent publication of a guide to more than two thousand eight hundred Mormon diaries and autobiographical accounts should force the historian to take a closer look at the patterns of motivation that operated below the surface of the well-organized trains with their captains of fifty and captains of ten.[40]

The refugee theme also appears in Texas history. Mark E. Nackman has analyzed Anglo-American migrants to Texas between 1821 and 1846 and found that the migration was spurred by the financial panics of 1819 and 1836, and that Texas was, in fact, an "escape hatch for debtors and other delinquents." "If Texas in its first generation of Anglo settlement can serve as an example of a western frontier community, it may be that the early West functioned as a receptacle for the gathering of much of the country's derelict population."[41]

By twisting Nackman's argument a bit one might apply his thesis to the forced removal of the Indian tribes west of the Mississippi in the 1830s and 1840s, the forced march of the Navaho from western New Mexico to the Pecos River Valley in 1862-1863, and the involuntary movement of scores of tribes to reservations in the West by 1890.

Not only was the involuntary population movement in the nineteenth-century Trans-Mississippi West enormous in volume, the fact that tens of thousands moved because of government policy, fear of jail, or fear of death, reveals a side of westering we did not fully comprehend even when we witnessed the movement of the Okies and Arkies to the Far West in the 1930s and the Black exodus from the South throughout this century.

Taken together, the immigration of several million people to the Great Plains, and other parts of the West between 1870 and 1900, and the constant internal migrations from region to region and town to town ever since, reminds one of vast tribal upheavals in Africa, so much so that one might define "pioneering" as being, in some instances, a form of hegira. One is also reminded that David Donald in describing the black Kansas Exodusters of 1879 said, "They were not migrants but refugees fleeing from oppression and bondage."[42]

Since the story of migration to the American and Canadian Great Plains between 1870 and 1900 will be handled in other sessions of this conference I will dwell on but a few aspects of that vast movement of peoples here. Suffice it to say that it, too, is a mixed story of success and defeat unforgettably punctuated by the weather, with good crop years between 1876 and 1887, and a decade of bad crop years until 1897. Out of these extreme conditions came the first realistic fiction about the frontier experience, a fiction that contained a new theme of gloom about the future of rural agricultural life.

At this point I would like to jump on a different horse for a moment and argue that whereas the novelists have understood both the positive and negative aspects of the Great Plains experience—one thinks of Willa Cather's strong Antonia, Per Hansa's powerful will, Old Jules's persistence, and Frederick Manfred's indomitable characters in his Siouxland series—the historians, from Walter Prescott Webb to W. Eugene Hollon, have stressed the aridity and failure of the region. In so doing they have made the West heroic through deprivation. They have failed, on the other hand, to see that persistence in the Plains has created the very toughness we think of as being truly Western. In his novel *On the Road*, Jack Kerouac makes the point I want to make:

> Eddie and I sat down in a kind of homemade diner. I heard a great laugh, the greatest laugh in the world, and here came this rawhide old time Nebraska farmer with a bunch of other boys into the diner; you could hear his raspy cries clear across the plains, across the whole gray world of them that that day. Everybody else laughed with him. He didn't have a care in the world and had the hugest regard for everybody. I said to myself
> WHAM
> listen to that man laugh. That's the West, here I am in the West.43

A similar basic good nature pervades ranchwoman Nannie Alderson's autobiography, *A Bride Goes West*.44 Mrs. Alderson, like thousands of other men and women on the Plains, persisted through incredible hardships and a notable fall in status, but came to an understanding of the landscape that approached grudging affection. Basically my argument is that out of this persistence you have the makings of a tough regional culture which is not just a product of farming or ranching, or of men and women against the weather. It comes from the people themselves. As Eli Mandel has noted: "To see regional man is not just to see him responding to environmental influence, but it is to observe him searching for a structure of meaning." Persistence, writes Peter Decker, is the key to the takeover by the foreign-born of the mercantile world of San Francisco.45

At the same time there are other sides to the Great Plains experience which we as historians or novelists have not explored adequately, namely the floating migratory labor pool that has existed since the days of bonanza farming, when thousands of urban folk from

St. Paul and lumberjacks from the North Woods came west to harvest grain in the summer and fall. There was a Canadian equivalent of this phenomenon that James Gray calls "the 1,000 mile excursion from Ontario." Meanwhile the floating population of cowboys roamed up and down the Great Plains grasslands with cattle herds, and Mexican workers crossed the border to lay railroad tracks across the West. Out of these disparate groups a permanently landless population of migratory workers has emerged which we see as deprived. But this form of unsettlement, now a century old, again suggests negative meanings for the theme of mobility which we have not paired with the positive ones. But, as we shall see, it might also suggest that mobility is a normal rather than an abnormal state of things.

Reviewing the phenomenon of American migration to the Trans-Mississippi West since 1898, Gerald Nash has estimated that forty million Americans and six million foreign-born peoples poured into the region between then and 1970 bringing with them eastern values, a faith in science and technology, entrepreneurial skills and the national crises of war and depression.[46] Here again we see the juxtaposition of voluntary and involuntary mobility. Between 1898 and 1914, for example, the Far West experienced a migration of wealthy New England and New York people seeking good climate. After 1905 there was a surge of middle class retirees from the Middle West. They were followed by a giant wave of lower middle class people from the Middle West and the southern and border states hunting both jobs and climate. By the 1920s the first large mass of Mexican immigrants had arrived in the Southwest.

Although this multiple population movement produced booms all over the West, this migration also marked the beginning of the unsettling of the West, for the large majority went to towns rather than to farms, and the Great Plains and Mountain states began to show signs of population decline. That decline became a rout in the 1930s when three hundred and fifty thousand Dust Bowl victims came to California seeking homesteads in a state already converted to corporate, mechanized farming. Of the four hundred and sixty-five thousand coming to the Pacific Northwest, on the other hand, many were younger, misplaced farmers of whom 85 percent were under forty-five years of age. Some came because of the Great Plains crop failure, some for jobs, and some for the climate.[47] Meanwhile a half million Mexicans came into Texas to work crops while California was busy exporting Mexicans. We are also beginning to discover that of the millions of tramps "on the road" in the 1930s, an alarming proportion—perhaps over a million—were boy and girl tramps.

While World War II restored prosperity to the West—the war was, in fact, the greatest event in Western history since the gold rush of 1849—the population movement out of the Plains and into the cities continued at a speeded-up pace. This time all sectors of the population were set in motion at once: Blacks from the South to California, Mexicans from Mexico, Anglo-Americans from all over, and the one hundred and twelve thousand Japanese who were evacuated from the West Coast involuntarily. After the war the boom continued. By this time the intellectuals, the scientists, and the professional classes had discovered Berkeley, Stanford, and the Southwest. The ingredients for a new urban West had been assembled as early as 1960.[48]

What does all this suggest besides the obvious fact that Americans continue to move about in extraordinary numbers? It should suggest as well that the unsettlement of the American West appears to be an even more profound event than its initial settlement. For such a conclusion I am indebted to Peter Decker of Duke University who is now working on a study of the urbanization of rural America. In a recent paper Professor Decker estimated that between 1929 and 1960 thirty million people have moved from farm to town, and that between 1960 and 1970 the number of farms has decreased by nine hundred thousand. If that trend continues only thirty thousand farmers will be needed to supply the agricultural needs of the United States in the year 2000. He also notes that the trend is accompanied by an increase in rural debt to the city and a real decline in farm income.[49] These statistics are dramatically underscored by the constant increase of rural ghost towns in both the United States and Canada. Richard Hugo's poem, "Map of Montana in Italy," captures some of the flavor of the new dispensation when he writes:

> With so few negroes and Jews
> We've been reduced to hating each other,
> Dumping our crud in our rivers
> Mistreating the Indians.
> Each year, 4000 more move,
> Most to the West
> Where ocean currents keep winter in check.[50]

Such incredible migration to the cities marks not only the defeat of pioneering, but of rural culture itself as a part of the national character.

The unsettling of the American West means crossing a social frontier into a world we have not begun to fathom.

As I look across the border to the Canadian Plains I am impressed that many patterns of settlement and mobility are similar to those of the American Plains. Beginning in the late nineteenth century an impressive number of people came into and out of the Prairie Provinces, among them perhaps as many as a million and a half Americans. In both regions the railroad preceded agricultural settlement, and similar booms and recessions occurred in the agricultural areas of each. In Palliser's Triangle Canada had its own Dust Bowl, and the Mennonites and other immigrant groups are examples of refugee rather than voluntary settlers. There is also a similar movement from country to town in both countries.

But there are differences as well. While Sir John Palliser and others gave the Canadian Plains a distinct character and warned man to adapt to it—just as Major John Wesley Powell did for the arid regions of the United States—there has been no Canadian Frederick Jackson Turner to elevate the process of pioneering into a mystique about the national character of Canada. This absence has allowed Canadian scholars and observers to discuss plains settlement in freer terms, as is evidenced in the impressive nine volumes on *Canadian Frontiers of Settlement*, edited by Mackintosh and Joerg in the 1930s. These and later studies do not appear to be overlaid with a sense of manifest destiny, the burden of theory, or the self-consciousness of Walter Prescott Webb's regionalism. Thus Kay and Moodie in their essay, "Geographical Perspectives of the Canadian Plains," find that the isolation of the Plains has produced a sense of place.[51] Others point out that many of the prairie pioneers came from urban backgrounds and upon arrival soon demanded the comforts and amenities of town life.[52]

A study of the original pioneers in the Peace River District by C. A. Dawson suggests that the operators and homemakers were heterogeneous in respect to birthplace, but that all exhibited "a marked residential mobility." Dawson found that "a few had moved from their boyhood homes to the region, but the great majority made two, three, four or five moves before they made their homes in the far north agricultural area." "We found many operators who had 'tried it out' for a time on practically every new agricultural frontier in the Great West, north and south of the international boundary line."[53]

One might attribute such mobility to a class of adventurers or drifters, but it apparently affected everyone. Henry Loucks, the Canadian-born son of an Irish mother and a Luxembourg father, moved to the States as a young man, served as a merchant, became enamoured of farm life and wound up as the editor of the *Dakota Ruralist*, as well as the foremost Populist leader of the state. Similarly Canadian-born Sockless Jerry Simson, one of American Populism's most colorful characters, first became a Granger in the Middle West, then a farmer and rancher in Kansas, and then after a brief career as a Populist Congressman, moved to a ranch in New Mexico.[54]

Dawson discovered in the Peace River District that pioneer settlers also had held many kinds of jobs and some had been in five other occupations before turning to farming.[55] This jack-of-all-trades quality is precisely the characteristic Americans identify with pioneering, with being a cowboy, or as an example of American "know how." In perspective it seems more an attribute of youth as well as being the way many nineteenth-century people sought to find themselves. The college student who works in a broker's office one summer, Glacier National Park the next, and on a road gang in New Jersey in his senior year, does not seem to be all that different from his wandering grandfather.

The whole process of both urban and rural boom and bust in the Canadian Plains in this century is captured, for me at least, in James Gray's splendid book, *The Winter Years*.[56] Gray, whose own career was that of a jack-of-all-trades workman and broker's clerk before becoming a reporter, is both observer and victim in the account. In the boom years before World War II, Gray, a resident of Winnipeg, found the job market so favorable that "jobs themselves were adventures to be savored." One could walk from one on to a new one; boomers could go from town to town, and the building tradesmen could work on the prairies in the summer and work in California in the winter. "Risk taking for the sake of risk had an endless fascination for Westerners," writes Gray.[57] Here Gray adds a factor which I think has been left out of the California story and the Great Plains experience by most historians who see settlers as passive recipients of bad luck and hard times, and as being innocent and parochial. When the depression came to Winnipeg, and to the Plains Provinces, one continues to find in Gray the good humor we find in Nanny Alderson and Kerouac's Nebraska farmer.

But even Gray says that "there were worse things than being on relief in Winnipeg, and worst of all was being a farmer in 'the Dust

Bowl'." The exodus from that region of the Canadian Plains had been going on since the 1920s, began anew in 1931, and was a flood by 1935. "Most of us in the cities," writes Gray, "were only vaguely acquainted with the extent of the disaster in the country. The story was too big to comprehend. As early as 1931 there were one hundred and twenty-five thousand destitute farm people in Saskatchewan alone."[58] But those days also passed and now Americans watch enviously as the three Plains Provinces leap to the front in oil, grain, coal and a score of basic products.

What are we to make of all these goings and comings in western North America? First of all it seems to me that the trauma of the overland trails is repeated to some degree in all subsequent migrations whether voluntary or involuntary, Canadian or American. To understand these later migrations—that is to say the phenomenon of mobility —to comprehend the personal male and female as well as the group response to migration, is to begin to understand the most continuous theme in the history of our two Wests. If there are no diaries and journals to tell the story then the novelist and the historian must penetrate this region of the mind for us. It is a story too powerful to be told in statistics. In the process they must also tell the saga of the unsettling of the West as effectively as they have told the story of pioneering and settlement. In some ways it must be a tragic account, not only because of the instances of failure through mobility, but because urbanization is wiping out the accomplishments and culture of those who did persist on the land and succeed.

A major chapter in that story should deal with the coming of American youths to Canada to escape the Vietnam War. It may well be that their letters and diaries, angry, guilt-ridden, full of frustration will be the equivalent of the literature of the gold rush, or, as a region of the mind, an equivalent of the literature of despair coming out of the depression-ridden Great Plains.

But perhaps we might end on a less gloomy note. Wandering people have a way of creating their own myths, of organizing the most deprived past into some meaningful thing, and of seeing values arising out of their failures. There is a culture even in the mobility of defeat. A little Japanese girl, removed from her home in California to a desert camp in Utah with her parents in 1941, wrote in her diary about the government barracks assigned them. It was, she said in ecstatic tones, "our new home." It is this expectation that makes mobility so fatally attractive, so much an aspect of both the American and Canadian tradition of crossing frontiers wherever they can be found. Whether it results in success or failure, it is one key to the culture of our two Wests.

Notes

1   Earl Pomeroy, "Toward a Reorientation of Western History: Continuity and Environment," *Mississippi Valley Historical Review*, XLI (March 1955).

2   Richard Allen, ed., *A Region of the Mind: Interpreting the Western Canadian Plains* (Regina, 1973).

3   Allen, pp. 201-209.

4   Donald Greene, "Western Canadian Literature," *Western American Literature*, II:4 (Winter 1968), 257-280; and Greene, "A Breakthrough into Spaciousness: The Collected Poems of Donald Davie," *Queen's Quarterly*, LXXX:4 (1973), 601-615.

5   As quoted in Greene, "Breakthrough into Spaciousness," p. 615.

6   John D. Unruh, *The Plains Across: The Overland Migrants and the Trans-Mississippi West, 1840-1860*, 2 vols. (Ann Arbor: University Microfilms, 1977), I:2. (Forthcoming as a book from University of Illinois Press, Urbana, 1978.)

7   David M. Potter, ed., *Trail to California: The Overland Journal of Vincent Geiger and Wakeman Bryarly* (New Haven, 1945).

8   John Phillip Reid, "Paying for the Elephant: Property Rights and Civil Order on the Overland Trail," *Huntington Library Quarterly*, XLI (November 1977), 37-64.

9   Benjamin B. Harris, Account of a Journey to the Gold Mines, 1849, p. 22. Ms. in H. E. Huntington Collection (HEH).

10   Daniel J. Levinson, "The Mid-life Transition: A Period of Adult Psychosocial Development," *Psychiatry*, 40 (May 1977), 100.

11   Helen Marnie Stewart, *Diary—1853* (Eugene, Oregon, 1961), p. 9. Charlotte Emily Stearns Pengra, *Diary—1853* (Eugene, Oregon, n.d.; reproduced by the Lane County Pioneer-Historical Society), p. 2; Mary Stuart Bailey, Journal 1852, entry for May 17. Ms. in HEH.

12   Philip A. M. Taylor, "Emigrants' Problems in Crossing the West," *University of Birmingham Historical Journal*, V (1955), 83-84.

13   Stewart, *Diary—1853*, p. 18; Charles G. Gray, Journal of An Overland Passage from Independence . . . in 1849, 2 vols., p. 69. Ms. in HEH.

14   Georgia Willia Read, ed., *A Pioneer of 1850, George W. Read, 1819-1880* (Boston, 1927), pp. 51-52; Mrs. Catherine Margaret Haun, A Woman's Trip Across the Plains in 1849, p. 17. Typescript in HEH.

15   L. N. Weed, Narrative of a Journey to California in 1849, p. 37. Ms. in Yale University Western Americana Collection (YWA).

16   Douglas S. Watson, ed., *The Santa Fe Trail to California, 1849-1852. The Journal and Drawings of H. M. T. Powell* (San Francisco, 1931), p. 45.

17   Lillian Schlissel, "Diaries of Women on the Overland Trail," p. 5. Typescript copy provided by author. See also published version in *American Studies*, XVIII:1 (Spring 1977), 87-100.

18   John M. Faragher, "Midwestern Families in Motion: Women and Men on the Trail to Oregon and California" (PhD Thesis, Yale University, June 1977).

19   Seth K. Humphrey, *Following the Prairie Frontier* (Minneapolis, 1931), p. 244.

20   Wallace Stegner, *Wolf Willow* (New York, 1962), pp. 287-288.

21   Howard R. Lamar, "Rites of Passage: Young Men and Their Families in the Overland Trails Experience, 1843-1869," essay to be published by the Charles Redd Center (Provo, Utah, 1978).

22   James G. Malcolm, Letters to Sara E. Malcolm, 1849-1852. Ms. in State Historical Society of Wisconsin.

23   Captain David DeWolf, Diary of the Overland Trail, 1849, and Letters, 1849-50. Typescript, Newberry Library. See especially, DeWolf to Matilda DeWolf, Sacramento City, July 30, 1850.

24   John A. Johnson, 1849 Manuscript. Ms. in YWA.

25   Kevin Starr, *Americans and the California Dream, 1850-1915* (New York, 1973), p. 52.

26   Rudolph M. Lapp, *Blacks in Gold Rush California* (New Haven, 1977), p. 272.

27   Lapp, p. 244.

28   Lapp, pp. 116-117.

29   Peter R. Decker, *Fortunes and Failures: White Collar Mobility in Nineteenth Century San Francisco* (Cambridge, Mass., 1978), p. vii.

30   Decker, Chapter 3, but especially 71-86.

31   Decker, pp. 168-193 passim.

32 Decker, pp. 253-255.

33 Pomeroy quoted in Decker, *Fortunes and Failures*, p. 255.

34 Pomeroy in Decker, pp. 250-260.

35 Robert H. Walker, "The Poets Interpret the Western Frontier," *Mississippi Valley Historical Review*, XLVII:4 (March 1961), 626.

36 Walker, 626 ff.

37 Walker, p. 630.

38 Walker, p. 630.

39 Wallace Stegner, *The Gathering of Zion. The Story of the Mormon Trail* (New York, 1964), p. 1.

40 Bitton Davis, ed., *Guide to Mormon Diaries and Autobiography* (Brigham Young University, Utah, 1977).

41 Mark E. Nackman, "Anglo-American Migrants to the West: Men of Broken Fortunes? The Case of Texas, 1821-46," *Western Historical Quarterly*, V (October 1974), 455.

42 David H. Donald, *New York Times Book Review*, January 30, 1977.

43 Jack Kerouac, *On the Road* (New York: Viking Press, 1959). Nebraska Dateline.

44 Nannie T. Alderson and Helena Huntington Smith, *A Bride Goes West* (Lincoln, Nebraska, 1969).

45 Allen, *A Region of the Mind*, p. ix; Decker, *Fortunes and Failures*, p. 250.

46 Gerald D. Nash, *The American West in the Twentieth Century* (Englewood Cliffs, New Jersey, 1973), pp. 2-3.

47 Nash, pp. 148-156.

48 Nash, pp. 195-219 passim.

49 Peter R. Decker, Seminar, National Humanities Institute, Yale University, April 5, 1978.

50 Richard Hugo, *The Lady in Kicking Horse Reservoir* (New York, 1973), p. 3.

51 B. Kaye and B. W. Moodie, "Geographical Perspectives on the Canadian Plains," in Allen, *Region of the Mind*, p. 28.

52 American Geographical Society, *Pioneer Settlement. Cooperative Studies by Twenty-Six Authors* (New York, 1932). See C. A. Dawson, "The Social Structure of a Pioneer Area As Illustrated by the Peace River District," p. 48.

53 Dawson, pp. 46-47.

54   "Henry Loucks," in *Reader's Encyclopedia of the American West*, ed. Howard R. Lamar (New York, 1977), p. 680; "Jerry Simpson," in Lamar, ed., pp. 1113-1114.

55   Dawson, pp. 46-47.

56   James Gray, *The Winter Years. The Depression in the Prairies* (Toronto, 1967).

57   Gray, pp. 5 ff.

58   Gray, pp. 161, 165.

Response: The Unsettling of the American West: *The Mobility of Defeat*

Earl Pomeroy

As in writing about Western-American territories Howard Lamar has gone beyond the bare bones of political structure and conflict to the social setting and sometimes anti-social greed of politicians, in giving us a preview of his work on migrants on the overland trails and putting their experiences in perspectives that incorporate Canada as well as the United States, and the twentieth century as well as the nineteenth, he has invited us to take new looks that could occupy us long past this session and this conference. The occasion is appropriate for his appeal, in a gathering more literary than historical. Though nineteenth-century poets dwelt as euphorically as historians on the contacts of pioneers with their physical environment, in describing character and personality and personal responses to migration, novelists have called attention to dimensions of stress in Western life as most historians have not, even while historians have more fully enumerated both failures in achievement and failures in character in contrast to the dominant theme of success, giving glimpses of "nasty buzzard's puke," in the language of Howard's emigrant, as well as eagles' wings. It is time for historians to catch up with the novelists, with Rolvaag and with Frank Norris; it is chastening to reflect that the one historian who has most clearly caught up with them on their own ground came to history out of literature: Carey McWilliams, who wrote several accounts of agribusiness and migrant labor while the agribusinessmen were still complaining about *The Grapes of Wrath*. (While appreciating McWilliams, one may footnote the impact of John Steinbeck by recalling that when the wife of a California legislator took up pen to defend the ranchers she did so in fictional form, in a novel soon mercifully forgotten except for its title, *Of Human Kindness*.)

While as an explorer of the recent West I particularly appreciate
Howard's insights into the era of the great migrations from Western
farms to cities, I hope that another time he will refer also to those early
frontiers where most migrations were shorter than those after 1849 but
also more likely to be permanent, the separation of the emigrants more
traumatic. The discovery of gold invited brief forays to gather fortunes
to be spent at price levels more normal than those of California, or
simply "to see the elephant"; steamships and soon railroads made the
round trip relatively manageable despite the titillating prospects of
brushes with Indians on the way, which, as George Stewart noted in
writing on the California trail, he did not find in overland diaries in
the classic form of attacks on beleaguered wagon trains. The Argonauts,
like their progenitors, intended to return; they left hostages at home
in property, family, and their own loyalties and expectations. It is
probably true, as Peter Decker has suggested, that they should have
gotten ahead more easily by remaining in the East than by going West.
But for most of them to have known that might have made little
difference, since they did not think or acknowledge that they were
moving permanently; the choice was not between East and West but
between the East after a visit to the West and the East without that
brief interruption. At another time they might have foreseen the
consequences of what they were doing more clearly, faced more squarely
why they left jobs and families, including the possibility that they had
failed at both.

The prominence of marital discord on the frontier, despite the
convention of the happy Western rural hearthside, invites us to look
further at marriage and the strains on it before and after the great
overland migrations, in turning with Howard from the confrontation
of Westerners with their physical environment to their confrontation
with each other and themselves. Respecting the forbearance of women
who gave up family, friends, household goods and the education of
their children, we may wonder how much trouble their husbands had
given them before they left home. Were there more broken marriages
in the West than in the East, or did the breaks simply become more
visible, without relatives at hand to discourage formal breaks and to
provide material as well as psychological support? Was the Western
environment as conducive to freedom for women as the new industrial
environment of the East, according to Edward Shorter's interpretations,
or did the most significant breaks sometimes occur, like David Levinsky's
fall from orthodoxy, before women and families moved west? Were
emigrants prone to failure both in marriage and at work?

There must have been remarkable strains on women and men
alike, though especially on women, in relations with neighbors in the
rural Far West. Though Turner called the sub-humid West the "social
frontier," and armchair sociologists and promoters described new
neighborliness in irrigation communities and in the ranch country,
Isaiah Bowman exposed an old secret when, interviewing ranchers in
Colorado and western Nebraska in the early 1920s, he found that they
seemed to extend hospitality to him in part because he was a stranger,
and that they commonly hated their neighbors. Perhaps they hated
them all the more because in their isolation they needed them, and had
few alternatives to depending on them.

One obvious alternative was, of course, moving to town, as
many rural Westerners did even before American farm population
peaked and began to decline in the 1920s, and where many emigrants
had lived—in much of the American Far West *most* emigrants—before
many of them took up farming. Rural sociologists concluded long ago
that cattle and wheat ranchers made the move chiefly to provide a
better educational opportunity for their children, and that most were
satisfied that they got it, since few returned even after alarms over
busing. But we do not know how unsettling an experience life in a
Western town or city has been, to borrow a term from Howard's title,
or what the residents lose along with what they gain. The other side
of opportunity or mobility can be uncertainty. Shortly before the
riots at Watts in 1965, Robert Q. Wilson pointed out that geographical
mobility—lack of ghettos in familiar form—gave the illusion of social
mobility that did not exist in Los Angeles, and that believing it existed
could cause an individual frustration about his failure to realize the
opportunities he thought he had, and inhibit political organization,
allowing discontent to build up without normal outlets. There is
evidence of tension among the rich as well as among the poor: elites
have been fluid enough to arouse anxiety about who belonged to them
or at least who was acceptable to them, as well as respect for them. The
recent publication of the diary of Judge Matthew Deady of Portland
has shown how a man who was wealthy, eminent in his profession,
and a leader in politics and in higher education, could worry about
social status enough to record carefully who was invited to major social
events and who was not. Not all political or economic tycoons felt so
secure as Senator George Hearst of California, father of the publisher,
who apparently enjoyed the gossip about his crude ways, saying,
"They say I spell bird b-u-r-d. Well, if b-u-r-d don't spell bird, what
the hell does it spell?"

Yet we could make too much of the strains of life in Western cities, as in any cities. I am not sure about the argument of my colleague, Dick Brown, that it was primarily the frustration of failure that led merchants to join vigilance committees, though they might join to drive out elements unwelcome on economic grounds; for some of them, joining followed on calculated conclusion that their stakes in a community were likely to last long enough to justify diverting time from short-range to long-range investments, and so from their most immediately private affairs, and on a sense of community, however limited to that sense of interest, with at least some of their neighbors. Many of those who did fail should not have been altogether surprised. As Robert Dykstra and Gunther Barth have shown, businessmen in new cities commonly were ready to cut and run, keeping their commitments well hedged, despite the puffing of town-site promoters. As they discovered the possibility that they themselves might fail, they wasted few tears on the failures of others, which were often opportunities to buy at distress prices, as for instance Henry Miller did in buying up land in California. They were less interested in recapturing the advantages that the successful won for the benefit of those who had failed or for the benefit of society as a whole. Henry George came closer to winning in New York City than in California or any other Western state.

Further, the fluidity and uncertainty of economic life in Western cities did not necessarily mean that the people who lived in them missed the social arrangements and relationships of older communities. I recall no women in San Francisco, Denver, or other Far-Western cities who wrote of missing the household responsibilities of their former homes; rather, they sometimes recounted the advantage of living in hotels, without having to worry about the servant problem, and clearly enjoyed the appearance of station that residence at the Palace or the Brown Palace conferred. Moreover, many of them had relatives close by, as Howard has suggested. Many years ago, Scott Greer undertook to study working-class life in the land of the freeway, Los Angeles, as a case study in chaotic individualism; he ended by demonstrating the closeness of family ties, discovering that the drivers of cars in traffic jams were not fleeing from social responsibility or discharging their sense of rootlessness but going to visit their relatives.

While tantalizing us, Howard promises also to give us, after the conference, the benefit of the full text of his paper, with footnotes, to ruminate over and to show to our students or to palm off as our own suggestions to them. Then we may forget our own failures, or mine, to respond in kind to him.

Prairie Settlement:
Western Responses in History and Fiction; Social Structures in a Canadian Hinterland

Lewis G. Thomas

The two sub-titles of this paper require some explanation. The first, "Western responses in history and fiction" was that originally announced. It arose out of my desire to explore my uneasiness with the image of Canada's prairie west presented in much of the writing about that region, and widely accepted as realistic both within the region and beyond its borders. As my explanation proceeded it became apparent that to keep the paper within reasonable dimensions and at the same time to achieve some degree of comprehensiveness was a task beyond my capacity. Indeed reflection brought a salutary realization of the dimensions of Western Canadian writing and the cursory nature of my acquaintance with it. What seemed to remain was a sense of conflict between a widely accepted view of the nature of prairie society and the realities of western Canadian social structures. This brought me to my second sub-title, and it is to the social structures of the west that most of my paper is directed. There is, I think, in the tension between these two sub-titles, between the perceptions of a society and its realities, an aspect of western history that could be usefully examined. Do the discomforts of living in a society that suffers from a widespread delusion about its nature affect the way in which that society's denizens write about its experience?

Some of the words used in this over elaborate title require some explanation. In the first place the word "prairie" needs definition, or at least an explicit recognition of its imprecision. It is not used here in the way in which a geographer would use it. It does not denote simply a physiographic region with peculiar physiographic features. It is used simply as a convenient term to comprehend three provinces of Canada that happen to have within their boundaries what the *Concise Oxford Dictionary* calls "large treeless tract[s] of level or undulating grass land." This is a highly unscientific use of the word but it is a use that, in the Canadian experience, has some historical and literary justification.

The word "settlement" is used here to embrace the process that established in the three prairie provinces a population predominantly of European ethnic origin. That process involves the native peoples as well as more recent arrivals. It is also used here to cover not merely the arrival in the region of a particular settler or group of settlers but also the experience of the settler and his descendants. It is necessary to notice not only the interaction between the settler and his environment but the nature of the society in which he was at once creator and modifier, and even a destroyer. Understood in this way "settlement" implies a continuing process. "Settlement" even in the narrow sense of establishing new communities in the wilderness, or in the slightly broader sense of assimilating existing communities to a norm established elsewhere, still continues, and is particularly evident in the north. The north is indeed a region that has a peculiar relationship with the prairie, as that word is used here. Much of the land of the prairie provinces, though much less of their population, is "northern" in an even more specific sense than that of most of the thickly populated areas of Canada as a whole. Professor W. L. Morton has maintained that Canadians are a northern people. The prairie provinces are certainly deeply involved with their north. Yet, in contrast with Ontario, Quebec and Newfoundland, the prairie west, like British Columbia, has not achieved political control of its adjacent northern hinterland. The Northwest Territories continue to exist only to the west of Hudson Bay and politically they are subordinate to Ottawa. From Victoria to Winnipeg there are no exact parallels to the northern roles of Toronto, Quebec City or St. John's.

"Western" is another word in my title which needs some comment. In Canadian terms "the west" certainly includes British Columbia. No resident of the prairie provinces would deny that British Columbia is part of the west but British Columbians, when they speak of the residents of Alberta, Manitoba and Saskatchewan, call them, not westerners, but "prairie people." Prairie people speak of a province largely consisting of mountains as "the coast." I defend my title by saying that even prairie people can have western responses. In my discussion of settlement I propose, not to exclude British Columbia, but to use her experience for purposes of comparison. For this distinction there are compelling historical reasons. When British Columbia entered Confederation she possessed, as a crown colony, an identity of her own, an identity comparable, at least in constitutional terms, with those of the Atlantic and central colonies, though of course not nearly so fully developed. Her entry was a matter of negotiation. The prairie provinces, and the Northwest Territories, were, on the other hand, created by the federal government. They were to be treated, not as colonies of Great Britain, but as colonies of a Canada dominated by the two central provinces. In contrast with British Columbia their lands, and all their natural resources, were controlled from Ottawa and used for national purposes until 1930, that is to say, all through the period of definitive settlement. Though the experience of British Columbia is parallel and complementary to that of her prairie sisters, it is different for constitutional and political reasons as well as for physiographic ones.

My title places a not altogether appropriate emphasis upon the word "responses." Western responses are very much a concern of this conference and I have something to say about them but the purpose of this paper is really more to attempt some description of the western society within which the western respondent lives or upon which he looks back as the ambience in which his view of the world was formed. There are of course many who concern themselves with the Canadian west in a literary way who would not necessarily see themselves as historians or writers of fiction. There are also those who write about the west, often with profound insight, who are not, or do not see themselves as, westerners either by upbringing or adoption. The purpose of this paper is not so much to describe, let alone analyse, individual responses, as to examine the society to which the individual responds. In such an examination it is sometimes necessary to distinguish between the realities of western society in the past and the way in which that past has come to be perceived. The Canadian west's perception of itself today is much encumbered by stereotypes, not all of them of native origin, but most of them built upon some aspect of western experience. The acceptance of these stereotypes dims the realities of the Canadian past, blurs the outlines as much of Canadian as of western identities, and, in the headlong rush of the post-industrial world towards homogenization, diminishes us at once individually and collectively.

The critical years of western settlement seem to me to be the half century that lies between 1870 and 1920, the years between the Canadian takeover of western British North America and the end of the Great War of 1914-18. These were the years in which the political, institutional and economic structures of the prairie west were established and the relationship of the region to the central government was firmly maintained. That relationship was essentially that of a colony to its metropolis. The role of the prairie west was to serve as the means by which Canada was to enter into the transcontinental heritage so fortunately preserved by the continuing British presence in northern North America after the War of American Independence. Unless this task of creative expansion was accomplished quickly and effectively, the vacuum to the west would be filled by the aggressive and dynamic republic to the south and Canada's national dream would be ended forever.

The achievements of Canada in the west, in what was not much more than two generations, were substantial. The resistance of Riel and his Metis was overcome. Lieutenant-Governor Archibald made a promising beginning in the reconciliation of the other Europeanized inhabitants of the Red River colony to the new regime. The Mounted Police carried law and order to the foothills of the Rockies, and, as the chief arm of the Canadian government, performed services to the emerging territorial community far beyond the normal demands of police duties. The Indians were assigned to reserves and the task of assimilating them to a settled society was left, one might almost say abandoned, to the missionaries. Governmental institutions were established for Manitoba and the Territories, and in 1905 Manitoba's second class provincial status was extended to Saskatchewan and Alberta. By 1885 a Canadian transcontinental railway system was in operation. Two more transcontinental systems emerged in the decade preceding the outbreak of war in 1914 and a network of branch lines spread across and beyond the populated areas of the prairies.

Settlement proceeded as the federal government elaborated this impressive infrastructure. Government also provided a land survey and a system for the allocation of land derived largely from the free homestead system of the United States but with some significant departures based on central Canadian and British imperial experience. For a generation the pace of settlement was painfully and disappointingly slow. The more promising farm lands of southern Manitoba filled up and, in the territory of Assiniboia to the west, farm settlement spread out from the Canadian Pacific's main line. In southern Alberta the ranching companies enjoyed their golden age on their bountiful leases but the population of the most westerly of the territories remained thin even in the most agriculturally favourable areas. Though Winnipeg began to see itself as at once the gateway and the metropolis of the west, Regina and Calgary were little more than the bases from which the federal government and the Canadian Pacific, institutions that were virtually indistinguishable, could assert their control over central Canada's hinterland.

Somewhere about the middle of the nineties of the last century the pace of settlement accelerated. Settlers began to pour in not only from central and eastern Canada and the United Kingdom but also from the United States and central and eastern Europe. The flood of immigrants, the provision of additional railway facilities and the end of the world depression of the latter part of the nineteenth century combined to produce for the prairie west not merely the promise of prosperity but an actual boom. The west, British Columbia as much as the prairies, could perceive itself, not as a neglected hinterland, but as the region that provided the dynamic base of a dynamic Canada, a Canada that, after a century of disappointments, could look forward to a century of expansion and progress comparable to that enjoyed by the United States. Those who had established themselves in favourable positions in the western polity could perceive themselves, not as a lonely and isolated garrison, but as the spear-head or the cutting edge of Canada's progress towards the final realization of her national dream.

The boom collapsed into recession in 1913 and the west went into the war years in a chastened, though still optimistic mood. The recovery of agricultural prices during the war was not sustained into the 1920s and the prairie west went into the long winter of discontent that was to last until the war of 1939-45 ushered in the period of comparative affluence that only in recent years has seemed to be more fragile than many Canadians believed. Three decades of relative prosperity have not wiped out the memories of the three decades of war and depression that followed the half century in which the process of prairie settlement was defined.

What was the nature of prairie society in this critical period of western settlement? In the first place it was a colonial society, living in a colonial polity, living with a colonial economy. Important decisions were made elsewhere. They were made by people who saw the development of the prairie west as a creative exercise of Canadian power in an empty hinterland, at its best in the interest of the people of Canada as a whole, at its worst in the interest of the business community of central Canada. Only secondarily, and generally very much secondarily, were the immediate interests of the people of the west given any recognition in major matters of national policy. It is, of course, only fair to say that generally government held that the decisions taken would be in the best long range interests of the western settler, an assertion which must have had a hollow ring for many of the members of the House of Commons from the maritime provinces. The fact that Canada was a democracy, and that the central government was concerned to provide democratic and representative local governments in the west, was of little consequence. The weight of population was always with Ontario and Quebec and the sphere of local government was limited, and especially limited in the prairie region while control of lands and resources remained at the centre.

Even those in the prairie west who occupied places of influence were in a subordinate position. Political parties, the federal civil service and the Mounted Police, the railways, to a large extent the churches, the banks, the administration of justice, even businesses, were in a dependent relationship to the metropolis. Though influential westerners might and did, as individuals, form part of the network that pervaded the Canadian structure and made it work, and though they might be able to exert some influence on policy through their manifold associations, the decisions that they implemented were not in the last analysis theirs, or those that might have enjoyed the support of the majority of their fellow westerners. The decisions made in Ottawa at the instance of Montreal and Toronto were likely to be acceptable to them, but if they were not they had no option to giving them force. They could see themselves as colonizers, carrying the national dream to the hinterland, but as colonizers they served, and were expected to serve, the purposes of the centre. They were part of the national establishment, but their role was that of creative agents in the new society that establishment was bringing into being in the west. They were not expected to be policy makers.

That new society was to be formed in a mould acceptable to the elite of the central provinces. It found its ultimate inspiration in Britain, and particularly in an idealized version of the rural life of nineteenth-century England. To transplant the shires to Canada's prairie west, or even to the more promising climate of British Columbia, was a formidable and possibly an unrealistic undertaking. The life of a country squire was an elusive ideal, even in Ontario or the eastern townships of Quebec, but the dream still lives in the rural or semi-rural environs of Toronto and Calgary, and of Winnipeg and Edmonton.

The determination that the new society should be British was complemented by a still stronger and more forcibly expressed determination that the Canadian west should not go the way of the western parts of the United States. To exclude American influence from the Canadian hinterland was in the interest of the Canadian business community and this supported a resolve that the violence and brutality perceived as characterizing the American frontier should have no place in the peaceful and orderly society of the Canadian west. As the railway must precede settlement so law and established institutions should be in place not only to support the settler but to ensure that he accepted the social disciplines that lay beneath the British conception of freedom.

This emphasis on trans-Atlantic social ideals and this abhorrence of North American continentalism was, at the policy making level, most explicitly expressed during the long period of the Conservative party's dominance at Ottawa. After 1895 more was heard of another social ideal, that of a society resting, not upon an ordered hierarchy that included large land owners, but on the strong back of the yeoman farmer, with a sturdy settler and his family on every quarter section. Though more in tune with the populist attitudes of many who gave their support to Laurier and the Liberal party, subsequent experience was to show that policies related to this optimistic view of the agricultural potentialities of the west were even more productive of human misery than earlier attitudes that at least gave some scope for reasonable land use. The populist and more egalitarian ideal was indeed acceptable to the business community, whether in the counting houses of the east or in the Winnipeg grain trade, for it promised an enormous expansion at once of western production and the western market. Those in the west who were in positions of influence, if not caught up in the spirit of the great boom of the early 1900s, could console themselves with the reflection that they were at least comfortably in place, and with the hope that the institutional structures they had created could accommodate and control this unprecedented expansion. Until the outbreak of war in 1914 the influential minority in the west had little reason to suppose that the region would not remain peaceful, orderly and British.

What the influential minority did not sufficiently take into account was the fact that theirs was an immigrant society. Most societies can of course be so described, and certainly the older societies of Canada east of the Great Lakes. Immigration to the west, however, took place under peculiar circumstances. The definitive period of western Canadian settlement was relatively short. In fifty years the west passed from the appearance of an empty and barbarous wilderness to that of a settled society with the appurtenances of western European civilization. That the wilderness had not been quite empty and that the appurtenances were of a somewhat jerry-built nature were contradictions that the westerner of 1920 ignored without much reflection.

This hasty passage occurred in an era when rapid communication, the product of the railway, the steam-boat and the telegraph, had already revolutionized the world to which the west looked for its models. The western settler could maintain a contact with his homeland much more easily than the generations of North American settlers who had come before the early nineteenth-century revolution in communications. Indeed the very speed with which the west was settled was a function of the revolution. It was also a major factor in bringing into the realm of possibility the whole enterprise of building a new society in the west and in maintaining the control over it of the central authority. For no one in the west was this ability to communicate easily and quickly with his home base more significant than for the members of the influential minority.

The use of a term like "influential minority" suggests that the view of western society put forward here departs radically from the stereotype of western Canadian development that portrays it as wholly the work of the sturdy homesteader, drawn from the ranks of the needy and oppressed of the world, who created, by heroic toil and suffering, an egalitarian, classless and unstructured society. Such weaknesses as a society so envisaged might have resulted from restrictions placed upon it by forces external to it or from infections spreading out from less wholesome and self-sustaining structures on its periphery. This view of western society is at least as far removed from reality as the stereotype of western history that supports it. Though the latter gives some recognition to the colonial relationship of the west to central Canada it ignores the social objectives of the national government as completely as it does the attitudes of the creative minority who acted as that government's effective arm.

This stereotype also obscures the part played by what may be called the privileged settler. It in no way derogates from the accomplishments of the pioneer to say that some of the settlers of the formative years had advantages of birth, wealth and education that enabled them to make a distinctive contribution to the western polity. Certainly the policy makers of the first twenty-five years saw them as a valuable element in the kind of society they hoped would emerge. Such settlers, when they came from relatively privileged backgrounds in relatively structured societies, could be expected to support precisely the kind of society the central Canadian elite envisaged for the west. Even those whose advantages were comparatively modest might aspire to an improved position in their new homes.

The factor of aspiration, which is almost always recognized even in the crudest stereotypes of the immigrant, was certainly an important element in the motivation of the privileged. Their aspirations were linked to a highly romantic view of the west as a land of opportunity where the best of life in the British Isles or in eastern Canada could be realized without the restrictions imposed by the density of population and the scarcity and high cost of land. The vision of the west current among the advantaged was heavily oriented toward the outdoor life, and especially toward both work and pastimes closely related to horsemanship. The writings of the Irish poet Moira O'Neill, who was also, as Mrs. Walter Skrine, the wife of an early Alberta rancher, provide a sensitive response not only to the foothills landscape but also to the way of life of the golden age of what David Breen has called the Cattle Compact. Her view was one that could only be seen from the back of a horse and it is not surprising that, after the Skrines returned to Ireland and their house was set on fire during the Troubles, all that Mrs. Skrine thought to rescue was her side-saddle.

The love of equestrian pursuits did not preclude an attachment to other values the privileged minority might have in their baggage. The institutions of the new society were heavily influenced by their attitudes to the church, the school, the courts, the professions, the public service and the provision of cultural amenities. These attitudes they saw as British, whether they were imported directly from the British Isles or, at one remove, from the eastern provinces or other parts of the British Empire. The coincidence of their values and attitudes with the objectives of the policy makers and organizers of the western polity is a fact of considerable significance in the shaping of western Canadian society and for its relationship with the Canadian polity as a whole.

In the structured societies upon which the western societies were modelled, and from which most of the privileged settlers came, status was determined by considerations that were ultimately economic, but complicated over the generations by breeding and education. In dynamic and fluid societies like those of nineteenth century Britain and the eastern provinces of Canada, a high degree of social mobility existed and the definition of the limits of gentility was increasingly nebulous. The monopoly of influence by a single caste had indeed been broken but even in late Victorian and Edwardian Canada enough of a class structure survived to ensure that the genteel could and would reach out to the genteel to provide, as far as was possible, the same human support that arises out of policies promoting group settlements based on ethnic or religious affiliations.

This factor of social contiguity in promoting and reinforcing the values that the dominant element in central Canada sought to establish in its western hinterland deserves further exploration. Why, for example, was the confrontation endemic in the rancher-squatter relationship, and evident in southern Alberta from the earliest stages in the development of the Cattle Compact, so successfully contained? Was it because so many of the small stockmen who moved into the ranching country had a common background with the ranchers and shared their aspirations to a particular way of life and their ideal of a rural and structured society? The exploration of such a problem cuts across deeply entrenched stereotypes of western egalitarianism and the homogenizing effect of a harsh environment that erases every evidence of human distinctiveness. The very suggestion that some settlers in the west had privileges, privileges which proved an advantage rather than a handicap in making their adjustment to the western environment, provokes a hostile response on the assumption that such an assertion implies a defense of privilege by its beneficiaries.

These stereotypes are entrenched not only in the west's collective perception of itself, a concept perhaps too flimsy and evasive to be intellectually respectable, but in much popular writing about the west, including much of what passes as popular history. They have not been wholly absent from academic writing about the west, especially in the field called social science. The trend of academic historical research, however, seems to be towards their rejection and towards a representation of the west that is much more complex, much more shaded, and, to me, much more interesting.

In a structured society that has attained a degree of maturity the place of the individual in the hierarchy is relatively fixed. The characteristics of a member of the influential minority are recognizable in terms of economic and social position. Levels of education and manners in a broad sense imply an acceptance of a collective way of life, supported by the acceptance of a complex of values. In an immigrant society like that of the prairie west the structures did not exist, except in a rudimentary form in the Red River colony and in the fur trading society to which it was affiliated. To create structures similar to those existing in central Canada, and in an idealized Britain, was the primary task of the central government. It was apparent that such structures were not necessarily of compelling interest to many of the potential immigrants they hoped to attract. They turned therefore to those whose backgrounds would suggest that the structures assumed to be best would be congenial. The objectives of government thus gave an opportunity to the privileged settler to move into an influential position and to use that position to realize aspirations that were coherent with the purposes of government.

When the pace of settlement began to quicken in the late nineties a western elite was in place, well established in cities like Winnipeg and Calgary, not to mention Victoria and Vancouver, and with significant connections in the rural west and in smaller centres, centres that might be resource based, like Lethbridge with its coal, or agricultural marketing centres like the towns of Assiniboia and Manitoba. Though the privileged settler was very much in a minority among the new arrivals of the boom years he reinforced and helped to develop the patterns of life he found already established. As he usually came from the eastern provinces or the United Kingdom his model of the good life was not much altered from that of an earlier generation. Though he might not have attained the material success of the established minority, he was more likely to aspire to association with the influential element than to seek to break its control. Easy communication with eastern Canada and the United Kingdom continued to support relationships with his home base and to promote entry into the associations, political and economic as well as cultural, that bound Canada together.

In this period of optimism about the western and the Canadian future, the beneficiaries of these associations were not inclined to denounce them as evidence of western subservience to the metropolis. During the war of 1914-18 no element in the west supported the Canadian war effort more strongly than the privileged settler. Even for those of the western elite who did not have the special concerns of the recent arrival from the United Kingdom, the disposition to make no distinction between a Canadian and a British cause was overwhelming. For the west, with its high proportion of young men and of recent arrivals, the war was an especially shattering experience, not only in its high casualty rates among a vitally important element in its population but also for its disruptive and destructive impact upon its relatively immature institutional structure. Though the elite's associations with Britain remained in working order, in the inter-war years they were no longer sustained by the infusion of privileged immigrants from overseas that had been so marked in the pre-war period. Though the world of the influential minority in the west was still London-centred and Americans remained suspect, its associations with central Canada assumed an increasing importance. Immigration in the twenties and the thirties no longer radically affected the patterns of settlement. There was in this period no major internal movement of the people comparable with the urbanization and rural depopulation that characterized the years after the war of 1939-45, though the drought and depression of the thirties did push many desperate farmers out of the stricken areas of the south. The influential minority became increasingly city based, though still maintaining its small town and rural outposts. A few of its affiliates were to be found in the popular movements that dominated prairie politics between the wars but the western establishment generally preferred to co-opt and tame the populist leaders. When leaders with recognizable establishment connections like Dufferin Roblin and Peter Lougheed appeared, western society was notably different from what it had been in the post-immigration period between the wars.

The western elite, whether in 1890 or in 1930, was a small minority in the total population of the region. In an immigrant society like that of the west in the settlement period, its values and attitudes were shared by many of the newcomers. It recruited itself easily, especially from the ranks of the privileged settlers. For its way of life it continued to look for its models across the Atlantic, or to eastern elites that looked in the same direction. It was increasingly urban and, in the larger cities, was concentrated in distinctly upper-class neighbourhoods, though its older generation was slow to leave the houses they had built close to the city centres. It continued to maintain social procedures that might have aroused more animosity had they been more conspicuous. It did not abandon its rural connections and these were reinforced by its continuing orientation towards outdoor sports. Its addiction to horses survived the automobile, and horse-shows, race meetings, and even polo, qualified the increasing addiction of the larger public to the rodeo. The west between the wars was by no means affluent and even the comfortably circumstanced on the whole refrained from the conspicuous consumption that is said to breed social hostility. Indeed the elite might almost be said to have pretended that it did not even exist, that its members were completely assimilated into the classless society of North America.

The structures of western society as they emerged from the painful decades of consolidation between the wars still reflected the social ideals and attitudes of the social planners and social engineers of post-Confederation central Canada. Yet whatever the attitudes of the elite, the political history of the period amply demonstrated the dissatisfaction of the majority of the prairie population with the region's continuing colonial relationship to central Canada. This dissatisfaction has usually been explained in terms of economic injustice, of which all westerners are equally the victims, and of the environmental hazards to which all westerners are impartially exposed. Yet in the kind of structured society that the west was meant to be, and did indeed become, the discriminations and divisions implicit in the structure imposed social discomforts that were likely to affect the individual response of the westerner to his society. Though the general acceptance of the pretense that the west was an egalitarian society veiled these internal frictions, this was no more effective in reducing them than the belief in Canada's essential democracy was in eliminating the strains imposed on the west by its colonial relationship to central Canada.

The affluence of the three decades that followed the war of 1939-45 profoundly affected the west. So did the changes in the world power structure as Canada perceived it. The predominance of the United States and the relative decline of Britain and France removed substantial obstacles to the penetration of North American continentalism. Nowhere in the west was this more obvious than in Alberta. The new wealth from oil and gas gave a new mobility within a society structured on the assumption of an agricultural base with all the limitations that implied. No matter how sedulously the elite had maintained its Canadian and trans-Atlantic associations, these had suffered and continued to suffer the attrition of generational change. Second cousins twice removed do not experience or maintain the intimacies of parent and child, or of brother and sister. Now these associations felt new pressures from outside. Calgary, even in the thirties the most English of prairie cities, became the most American. Edmonton, except in the university community less exposed to the assault from the south, was transformed into something resembling a cosmopolitan city under the influence of the new emigration from Europe. The new immigrants came, not to farm in ethnic groups, but to use their talents and their training in an urban environment. The old models of the good life, though they did not wholly disintegrate, were considerably modified by North American consumerism and aspirations to a style that was in its inspiration more international than purely British.

The post-war years raised the general level of material well-being in the west. This blurred the distinctions between the levels in its social structure, distinctions that were in any case yielding to the homogenizing tendencies of post-industrial society in North America and much of western Europe. Individual voices were raised to protest against injustice to groups like the Indians which had not conspicuously benefited from the pervasive prosperity, but the collective conscience of the west was not noticeably aroused. Official recognition that the west was now a multicultural society won a comfortable acceptance. Inequities within that society aroused far less interest than the region's continuing concern with its relationship to central Canada. The more conscious the west became of its comparative prosperity, the more it resented the retention of the power of decision by a more populous centre. This discrepancy in the location of political power and economic resources posed questions to the individual in the western society that were not wholly new but to which he had never before had to respond from anything resembling a position of strength.

The Fear of Women
in Prairie Fiction:
An Erotics of Space

Robert Kroetsch

How do you make love in a new country?

In an allegorical passage in Willa Cather's novel, *My Antonia*, we learn that two men who batch together on the Nebraska plains are the same Pavel and Peter who, leaving a wedding party in Russia, fed the bride to pursuing wolves. Pavel tells his story to the newly arrived immigrant, Mr. Shimerda, and shortly thereafter dies. The survivor, Peter, kisses his cow goodbye, eats at one sitting his entire winter supply of melons, and goes off to cook in a railway construction camp where gangs of Russians are employed.

Young Antonia translates the story of the devoured bride from its European languages into American, from adulthood into childhood, for her willing but naive listener, Jim Burden. She is, it turns out, posing for the potential writer and the potential culture of the Great Central Plains the question: How do you make love in a new country?

In a paradoxical way, stories—more literally, books—contain the answer. How do you establish any sort of *close* relationship in a landscape—in a physical situation—whose primary characteristic is *distance*? The telling of story—more literally, the literal closedness of a book—might be made to (paradoxically again) contain space.

Already the metaphor of sex, uneasily, intrudes. We conceive of external space as male, internal space as female. More precisely, the penis: external, expandable, expendable; the vagina: internal, eternal. The maleness verges on mere absence. The femaleness verges on mystery: it is a space that is not a space. External space is the silence that needs to speak, or that needs to be spoken. It is male.

The having spoken is the book. It is female. It is closed.
How do you make love in a new country?

Most books contain the idea of world. Not all contain the idea of book.
In those that contain both we get a sense of how book and world have
intercourse. Two such novels are Willa Cather's *My Antonia* and Sinclair
Ross's *As For Me and My House*. As paradigmatic texts in the literature
of the western plains, they discover its guises and its duplicities, its
anxieties and its accomplishments. They offer, finally, an erotics
of space.

Both fictions begin by pretending not to be fictions; they
conceal their artfulness by denying it. Cather's novel is supposedly an
unpublished manuscript, a personal reminiscence left with a friend who
might be male or female, who might be Willa Cather herself or a
character from the town in the reminiscence. Ross's novel is supposedly
a diary kept by the wife of a man who either was or wanted to be an
artist—but who failed, certainly, to write the book that he wanted
to write. This same failed book appears in many guises in Western
Canadian—if not Western American—writing: the failure of white man's
discourse in Rudy Wiebe's *Big Bear*, the anxiety about divination in
Margaret Laurence's *The Diviners*; or, farther west, the encounter with
muse and book in Robert Harlow's *Scann*. And possibly speaking the
concealed message for all of them is Lowry's *Under the Volcano* and
Geoffrey Firmin's failure to write the book that would restore magic to
a forsaken world and, thereby, potency in the face of the vengeful bride.

Willa Cather's male narrator, Jim Burden, recognizes that he
is somehow up against a bride-muse figure who cannot find an adequate
mate. Guided by the scholar and teacher, Gaston Cleric, he reads the
"Georgics" and meditates on Virgil's statement: "for I shall be the first,
if I live, to bring the Muse into my country." Then he meets Lena
Lingard, there in Lincoln, and is reminded of the laughter of the other
immigrant daughters—the hired girls—in Black Hawk. "It came over
me," he says, "as it had never done before, the relation between girls
like those and the poetry of Virgil. If there were no girls like them
in the world, there would be no poetry."

But how do you make love in a new country?

Gaston Cleric, the failed poet—the poet, incidentally, who talked his
talent away—discovers that young Jim is spending time with Lena.
"You won't do anything here now," he warns Jim. "You should either
quit school and go to work, or change your college and begin again in

earnest. You won't recover yourself while you are playing about with this handsome Norwegian. Yes, I've seen her with you at the theatre. She's very pretty, and perfectly irresponsible, I should judge."

That perfect irresponsibility might have been the making of a poet. Jim Burden, instead, heeds the lesson in fear of women. He leaves Lincoln and goes east. He will, thereafter and always, court the muse at a great distance.

Philip Bentley, on the other hand—the hero of Ross's novel — met the muse and married her. Mrs. Bentley is almost pure talk, pure voice, her husband almost pure silence. Yet it was not talk that led to their marriage, but music. Philip attended a recital to hear her play a rhapsody by Liszt. A *rhapsody*. "The desire to reach him," Mrs. Bentley tells her diary, "make him really aware of me, it put something into my hands that had never been there before. And I succeeded. He stood waiting for me afterwards, erect and white-lipped with a pride he couldn't conceal. And that was the night he asked me to marry him."[1]

Philip Bentley marries the muse and becomes, not a writer, but, if we are to believe the promise of the novel's ending, a dealer in secondhand books. Jim Burden meets the muse and flees and later travels for a great Western railway and writes a reminiscence. In both novels the essential awe that might have produced the great artist of this prairie space is distorted by a fear that exceeds the wonder. The male who should be artist is overwhelmed. The bride expects to receive as well as to give. How do you possess so formidable a woman?

By transgression. By substitution. . . . Philip Bentley cannot have a child by his wife; he has (apparently) a son by Judith West (and consider her last name; her *last* name), the farmer's daughter. That woman dies giving birth to her illegitimate son. Jim Burden, in approaching Lena Lingard, has already substituted her for Antonia Shimerda. Antonia has been got pregnant by a railway conductor; she is abandoned before the wedding; she, like Judith West, returns to the family farm—to the land and unmarried—to have her child.

The male is reluctant to locate and to confront the muse. He works by trespass. The writer becomes the thief of words. And his fiction—the book that conceals and denies its bookness—is written as much from fear as from love. The love of woman that traditionally shaped the novel—boy meets girl (and Cather plays with that tradition) —is violently rivalled by a fear of woman as the figure who contains the space, who speaks the silence. And the resultant tension determines the "grammar" of the western novel.

The basic grammatical pair in the story-line (the energy-line) of prairie fiction is house: horse. To be *on* a horse is to move: motion into distance. To be *in* a house is to be fixed: a centering unto stasis. Horse is masculine. House is feminine. Horse: house. Masculine: feminine. On: in. Motion: stasis. A woman ain't supposed to move. Pleasure: duty. The most obvious resolution of the dialectic, however temporary, is in the horse-house. Not the barn (though a version of resolution does take place there), but whores'-house. Western movies use that resolution. Sheila Watson treats of that resolution in *The Double Hook*. Antonia Shimerda is unhoused, almost into whoredom. Philip Bentley is unhorsed into housedom.

But the *hoo*-erhouse of western mythology is profane; against it the author plays the sacred possibility of the garden. Pavel and Peter, in Russia, might well have expected to recover their innocence by journeying to America. Even Jim Burden, American-born, playing in his grandmother's Nebraska garden, noticing the grasshoppers and the gophers and the little red bugs with black spots on their backs, can report: "I was entirely happy." Place is in many ways the first obsession of prairie fiction—a long and elaborate naming *takes place*; and one of the first attempts is the trying on of the name, Eden—even by a boy named Burden.

He and Antonia expect to find a natural version of that Eden in a dog-town. Jim is "examining a big hole with two entrances" when Antonia shouts something at him in Bohemian. "I whirled around," he reports, "and there, on one of those dry gravel beds, was the biggest snake I had ever seen. He was sunning himself, after the cold night, and he must have been asleep when Antonia screamed. When I turned, he was lying in long loose waves, like a letter 'W.' . . . He was not merely a big snake, I thought—he was a curious monstrosity. His abominable muscularity, his loathsome, fluid motion, somehow made me sick."

This time it is Jim who translates, violently, a European story into the New World. The Eve of this version shouts a warning. But her Adam says, petulantly, "What did you jabber Bohunk for? You might have told me there was a snake behind me!" The naming fails; the Freudian silence of America triumphs. Jim kills the snake with a spade. The boy and girl had ridden together to the dog-town on Jim's pony. Now that same Jim—or that "experienced" Jim—exultant at his kill, walks home carrying the spade and dragging the snake, with Antonia riding alone on Dude, the pony.

The geography of love and the geography of fear: on the prairies it's hard to tell them apart. And if Jim Burden has difficulty, the Bentleys of the Ross novel have even more. They are already in exile from anything resembling paradise when first we meet them, and Mrs. Bentley must come close to being the most incompetent gardener in all of fiction. Historically, the frontier had in a sense "closed" by the time the Canadian prairies opened to settlement. Significantly, the idea of garden finds its fullest expression at the end of the Cather novel, in the middle of the Ross novel.

Antonia, by the end of *My Antonia*, has in fact created an earthly garden of matronly delights. When Jim, in his hesitant way, visits the farm where Antonia now lives, he is taken almost immediately into the apple orchard. "In the middle of the orchard we came upon a grape arbour, with seats built along the sides and a warped plank table." Jim and Antonia sit down and watch the numerous children at play. "There was the deepest peace in the orchard. It was surrounded by a triple enclosure; the wire fence, then the hedge of thorny locusts, then the mulberry hedge which kept out the hot winds and held fast to the protecting snows of winter."

Antonia's husband, needless to say, is not at home. He is, we are told, "not a man of much force." Jim, in the disguise of "mere" description, can imagine he has come either to the Sleeping Beauty figure or to the *vagina dentata*—but not to a flesh-and-blood woman. He and Antonia for one last time sleep under the same roof—the artist again, by trespass, by subterfuge, by substitution gaining small access to his muse, remaining still and always the virgin, both feeding and feeding on his fear of the *woman*liness of woman, delighting in the near miss; lost pleasure becoming his secret pleasure. . . .

In the middle of the Ross novel, Philip and Mrs. Bentley take a vacation from the town of Horizon. Advised by Paul Kirby, the primal couple goes west to a ranch, intending to buy a horse for the boy they've taken into their house.

Kirby is a kind of parody-double of Philip, as Gaston Cleric is of Jim Burden. But this scholar-teacher-guide is addicted to words —simply to words—not to classical authors. He clings to the last hope of a naming. A man who studies sources, origins—it is he who directs the Bentleys out of town, back to nature.

"Just as Paul promised," Mrs. Bentley writes, "there are the hills and river and horses all right, but the trees turn out to be scraggly little willow bushes that Philip describes contemptuously as 'brush.'" The trees will not be The Tree. "With his artist's eye for character he says the best ones are the driftwood logs, come all the way from the mountains likely, four or five hundred miles west. They lie gnarled and blackened on the white sand like writhing, petrified serpents."

Paradise has once again retreated over the horizon and into the west. The snake in this place is seemingly older than the garden itself. And the labyrinth of naming and misnaming is complicated further by Paul's own boyhood fancy—he still insists that a hill across the river be called "the Gorgon."

The woman who is the centre and the power on the ranch is Laura, "A thorough ranch woman, with a disdainful shrug for all . . . domestic ties. There is a mannish verve about her that somehow is what you expect, that fits into a background of range and broncos . . ." This girlish-woman of forty-five was once a rodeo star. Her husband avoids her. She is almost the androgynous figure who exists prior to all coupling (or uncoupling), and the world she presides over is ambiguous indeed.

Here the women sleep in a house, under pictures of bulls and stallions; the three visiting men sleep, domestically, in a tent by the river. Mrs. Bentley pays a visit one night to the male territory, because it is "hot and close" in the house; but she cannot approach the males and their campfire; she feels her husband does not want to be "bothered" with her. She goes past the tent and the fire into a natural world that is as "unnamed" as the human configurations and relationships. Death and life, natural and supernatural, pagan and Christian, male and female, heaven and hell—her binary categories collapse. Like draws to like, she says, enigmatically, unable to make distinctions. The original place is chaos. Mrs. Bentley looks into that dark. With "a whole witches' Sabbath" at her heels, she makes a bolt for the house.

Mrs. Bentley, at least for the moment, returns to the house-horse dialectic. She feels relieved—at home even with the picture of a Hereford over her bed. Not until she has gone dancing will she notice that the cow is a bull, none other than (perhaps by an error in naming) Priapus the First.

Anyone who grew up on the Great Plains knows that the one night that offers a smidgen of hope for sexual harmony (be it ever so chaotic) is dance night. In a world where the most pleasurable activities—hunting, fishing, drinking, swearing, athletics, story-telling and work—are homo-erotic, the one occasion where men and women might freely "act" together is at a dance. There are dance scenes in both *As For Me and My House* and *My Antonia*.

The cowboys on the ranch take Philip to a bunkhouse and fit him out "in a dark blue shirt, ten-gallon hat and red silk handkerchief."

But Laura takes one look at him and says it's a pity he can't dance.

On this Saturday night a stripling cowboy, as tall as Philip, on a bet dances with Mrs. Bentley. He ends up taking her for a bite to eat (at the Chinaman's, I trust), and then for a walk to the outskirts of town to have a look at his horse—"Smoke, he called him, a little ghost-horse in the stray flickers of light from the street, a light mottled gray, with pure white mane and tail." . . . A minister's wife should know her pale horses when she sees one. She returns to the dance to find Philip back from his shopping, sprawled on a bench along the wall, the boy Steve asleep on his shoulder.

Young Jim Burden sneaks out of his grandparents' town house to go to the dances and worship the young women, the country girls who make the dances a success with their energy and enthusiasm. His grandmother finds out about his nightly activities. He ends up sitting "at home with the old people in the evenings . . . reading Latin that was not in our high-school course"—learning, by heart, a "dead" language.

The failure of the male protagonists, at the centre of each book, to enter into the dance, is symptomatic of what is wrong. The women can dance. Their appropriate partners cannot. The harmony suggested by dance—implications of sex, of marriage, of art, of a unified world—all are lost because of the male characters. The males are obedient to versions of self that keep them at a distance—the male as orphan, as cowboy, as outlaw.

Jim Burden leaves Virginia for Nebraska because he lost both his parents in one year. He reads a "Life of Jesse James" on the train, and finds it "one of the most satisfactory books I have ever read." His closest male companion on the homestead is Otto Fuchs, a cowboy who tells great tales of the frontier; an Austrian-born all-American cowboy who every Christmas writes a letter home to his ma. Jim acquires traits that are parallel to those of the cowboy, especially the ability to be both devoted and distant. And already in the introduction to his reminiscence he is a version of Jesse James; he works for a Western railway at a time when railways were not renowned for their integrity. He is somehow orphan, cowboy and outlaw.

The case of Philip Bentley is possibly more extreme. He was born out of wedlock, to a waitress whom he despises, out of a vanished father whom he admires. The house of his childhood is close to the horse/whores' house. The father (the Christian God?) is pure distance.

Philip, a version of the orphan, temporarily adopts the orphan Steve, whose mother abandoned him. Through the orphaned boy and Paul Kirby's faith in horses he has a shot at being a cowboy. But finally

he is mostly (or almost) an outlaw—against religion, against society—
even, in his silence, against art.

In the first paragraph of *House*, Philip Bentley has thrown
The male as orphan or cowboy or outlaw is drawn to and
threatened by the house. The house is containing, nurturing, protecting,
mothering. But the house is closed to the point where it creates, even
in Mrs. Bentley, a terrible claustrophobia.

Or perhaps her claustrophobia is a clue.

Both Mrs. Bentley and Antonia Shimerda, out on the plains,
are capable of doing both women's and men's work. Neither will,
finally, quite accept the assigned role—the assigned "name."

In the first paragraph of *House*, Philip Bentley has thrown
himself across the bed and fallen asleep, his clothes still on, one leg
dangling to the floor. He is both the spent man and the tired boy.
In the next paragraph his wife says: "It's been a hard day for him,
putting up stovepipes and opening crates, for the fourth time getting
our old linoleum down. He hasn't the hands for it. I could use the
pliers and hammer twice as well myself, with none of his mutterings
and smashed-up fingers either, but in the parsonage, on calling days,
it simply isn't done. . . . It was twelve years ago, in our first town, that
I learned my lesson, one day when they caught me in the woodshed
making kindling of a packing box. 'Surely this isn't necessary, Mrs.
Bentley—your position in the community—and Mr. Bentley such a big,
able-bodied man—'"

Granted, she takes the pliers to him a bit—recalling such an
incident twelve years after it happened. But she's in Horizon—a town
that is place and space at once, somewhere and nowhere, always present
and never to be reached. She has a problem in naming that persists
right through to the last paragraph of the book. And her problem is
that she is more than any of her names will allow her to be. She is as
much in need of a great artist—a great namer—as her artist is of a
great muse.

Antonia is sometimes called Tony. "Oh, better I like to work
out-of-doors than in a house!" she sings to young Jim Burden. "I not
care that your grandmother says it makes me like a man. I like to be
like a man." . . . Antonia refuses any mere role, any definition that is
less than the total, hurt dream of this total landscape. Song of myself
as everything.

By still another paradox, the male figure, out in this space, out
in the open, presumably free, once epic hero, is now the diminished
hero. The woman, in the age-old containment of house or town, is, in

prairie writing, the more-than-life figure—but one who is strangely sought.

How do you make love in a new country?

Curiously, travel becomes a second obsession in these place-obsessed books. Travel is possibly the true intercourse in these prairie novels: a frenetic going back and forth, up and down, in and out.

The Bentleys buy a horse from the ranch and bring it into town. The boy, Steve, riding and riding on the edge of town, acts out the ritual of desire and failure that is the life of his adopted parents. Mrs. Bentley, finally, is united with her husband in their mutual desire to travel to the city that is two hundred miles away. Antonia is got pregnant and deserted by a railway conductor. Otto and Jake, the boy-men of the Burden farm, must head out to open country when the family moves into town. Young Jim Burden and Gaston Cleric leave Nebraska to have intercourse with the East and Harvard. Tiny Soderball goes to the goldfields of the Yukon, where briefly she finds a true male friend—one who has no feet. The older Jim Burden, on his iron horse, wanders restlessly and endlessly across the continent, never forgetting his Antonia. Pavel and Peter, over and over, throw the bride to the pursuing wolves; and always they are pursued.

I think it would be naive to attribute the absence of explicit sex—of its language or its actions—merely to prudery on the part of either Cather or Ross; for the same absence is an operative presence in the works of numerous prairie writers. Space and place are not quite able to find equation. The men are tempted by friendship with other men, as in the opening of F. P. Grove's *Settlers of the Marsh*. The women are tempted by dreams of androgyny, even in a book as recent and as explicit and as travel-obsessed as Tom Robbins's *Even Cowgirls Get the Blues*.

Travel, for all its seeking, acts out an evasion. One can travel to the next room as well as to the far side of a continent. There is an absence of face-to-face confrontations in both *As For Me and My House* and *My Antonia*—either in the classic missionary position or in its verbal equivalent, the tete-a-tete. Mrs. Bentley, desperate, talks to herself through her diary. Jim Burden delivers his manuscript to the anonymous and sexless figure who opens the novel. In neither book are the written accounts read by the persons for whom they might have been intended. We have only the isolation of the self—the not being heard, the not hearing.

How do you make love in a new country?

It seems to me that we've developed a literature, on the Great Plains, in which marriage is no longer functional as a primary metaphor for the world as it should or might be. The model as it survived even in Chaucer (for all his knowledge of the fear of women), through the plays of Shakespeare, through the novels of Jane Austen and D. H. Lawrence, has been replaced by models of another kind. What that kind is, I've only begun here to guess.

The novels by Cather and Ross give us a clue with their demanding and deceitful titles: *My* Antonia, *My* house. For, in spite of the attempts at possession—in spite of the pretense at possession—we know that something else was the case. We cannot even discover who is protagonist: Antonia or Jim Burden? Philip or Mrs. Bentley? Male or female? Muse or writer? Horse or house? Language or silence? Space or book?[2]

This is a new country. Here on the plains we confront the hopeless and necessary hope of originality: constantly, we experience the need to begin. And we do—by initiating beginnings. We contrive authentic origins. From the denied Indians. From the false fronts of the little towns. From the diaries and reminiscences and the travel accounts. From our displaced ancestors.

Here, the bride, so often, without being wife, turns into mother. The male cannot enter into what is traditionally thought of as marriage—and possibly nor can the female. The male, certainly, to make his radical beginning, takes on the role of orphan or cowboy or outlaw. He approaches the female. He approaches the garden. He approaches the house. . . .

And only then does he realize he has defined himself out of all entering. If he enters into this marriage[3]—and into this place—it will be he—contrary to the tradition of the past—who must make the radical change. It will be he—already self-christened—and not the woman this time—who must give up the precious and treacherous *name*.

Notes

1   I ignore (evade, if you prefer) Mrs. Bentley's own need of a muse-figure—
    assuming that the performer of a musical composition is in as much need
    of inspiration as its composer. And, further, I ignore Ross's confrontation
    with music and art. The music comes from far places. The art (drawing,
    painting), in a manner that is characteristically Canadian, precedes both
    writing and music in its recognition of what is *present*.

2   By a final paradox, Cather and Ross give us magnificent books that are
    written about the fear that keeps writers from writing books. *My Antonia*
    is a novel about the making of art, against the talk of being artist: Cather's
    Jim Burden is married to a New York woman who acts as patroness in that
    "arty" world. *As For Me and My House* is a novel about the artist, against
    art. The naming has become a near impossibility. One can only *be* an artist;
    let the silence speak what it will.

3   I have, of course, made a "cowboy" reading of the texts at hand. I trust that
    Sandra Djwa will domesticate my wanderings with a Lady of the House
    reading.
            Further, and as an example of the sense of community inspired
    by the conference: Glen A. Love, of the University of Oregon, spoke to me
    after I'd presented this paper. He is writing on Cather, and certainly resists
    my theories: yet he referred me to an essay that would seem to give me
    support, and with a vengeance: Blanch H. Gelfant, "The Forgotten Reaping-
    Hook: Sex in *My Antonia*," *American Literature*, 43:1 (March 1971), 60-82.
            And, finally, I want to thank Ms. Patty Daneman, my research
    assistant at SUNY-Binghamton. She became, as we together revised this
    paper, my ideal reader.

Response: **The Fear of Women in Prairie Fiction: An Erotics of Space**

Sandra Djwa

It's hard to know how to respond to these . . . ejaculations.

Bob Kroetsch's argument, as I see it, runs something like this. The prairie writer's relationship is with space. But space is distant and it is difficult, if not impossible, to establish a close relationship with it. This can only be done through a book—for a book can contain space. "Somehow," Bob Kroetsch tells us, "we think of external space as 'male' and internal space as 'female.'" Within this structure, the appropriate metaphor for the creative process becomes sexual intercourse. Thus, the real question for the prairie writer is, "How do you make love (that is, write a book) in a new country?" Most books of Western Canada, he continues, are "failed books" and the writers' failure is "to write the book that would restore magic to a foresaken world and thereby potency in the face of the vengeful bride." The thesis is that Jim Burden of *My Antonia* and Philip Bentley of *As For Me and My House* are failed writers. They fail because of fear of the woman as muse. Kroetsch's glum conclusion is that "we've developed [in the West] a literature in which marriage no longer functions as a primary metaphor for the world as it is or should be."

There is much in this paper that I agree with. The prairie novel is characterized by a covert sexuality and I think Bob Kroetsch is right to instinctively fasten on the slight, but tantalizing reference to Philip as a failed author. I'm not sure, however, that "making love in a new country" is the right metaphor for the discussion because in application it imposes a particular post-sixties view of sexuality and the creative process on novels that were written under quite different premises and published as long ago as 1918 and 1941. Because of its metaphysics this paper becomes a kind of original composition which proceeds in terms of "charged" images. This results in a talk

that is bracing in style, full of imagistic wit, and fun to listen to—
I particularly like the horse-hooer-house puns—but it is not Willa
Cather's *My Antonia* nor Sinclair Ross's *As For Me and My House*.

Let's begin with the introduction to this paper, Cather's
curious story about Peter and Pavel. The story, told by the dying
Pavel, is about the return journey from a wedding in Bohemia—
a journey which ends in disaster when the party is pursued by a pack
of hungry wolves. As Bob Kroetsch reminds us, Peter and Pavel save
themselves by throwing the 'bride' to the wolves. But the story is
not quite as Bob tells it because the groom as well as the bride is
thrown to the wolves. Is this omission so very important? Well, yes,
perhaps so. Because if we have "bride," "death" and "wolves," we have
a group of images charged with negative meaning, images which provide
a foundation for a later argument that Antonia and Mrs. Bentley are
variants of the "vengeful bride." But if we have a situation where both
the bride and groom are thrown to the wolves we do not have an act
directed against the female but a crime against humanity at large.

And, indeed, returning to *My Antonia*, we find that Pavel
and Peter are ostracized by their countrymen in the old world as in
the new precisely because their action is a crime against humanity.
The two children, Jim and Antonia, listening to this tale in the new
world learn from the mistakes of two exiles from the old. Pavel's story
as translated by Antonia for Jim Burden becomes one of their first
bonds. Hitherto he'd taught her English and killed the snake that
menaced their prairie Eden (demonstrating, by the way, the essentially
sexless nature of their relationship), now she reciprocates with a tale
from her world which provides talk for a whole winter, emotionally
knitting them together. Rather than a woman emasculating a man as
an equivalent of the vengeful bride, Antonia quite literally becomes
Jim Burden's muse.

We are led to believe from Bob Kroetsch's paper that Jim
Burden failed to write his book. Yet, in fact, he did: it is Jim's book
which we now read as *My Antonia*. Similarly we are led to conclude
that Antonia fails as muse because she is not a compliant sexual
partner. Yet Cather is reaching back to a much older image of woman
as muse, an image that Spenser or Dante would have understood:

> "Do you know, Antonia," says Jim, "I'd like to have you for
> a sweetheart, or a wife, or my mother or my sister—anything
> that a woman can be to a man. The idea of you is a part of
> my mind; you influence my likes and dislikes, all my tastes,
> hundreds of times when I don't realize it. You really are a
> part of me."

Jim and Antonia, siblings in childhood, can never be lovers. But
Antonia is nonetheless the woman as muse. Here is Jim's description:

> She lent herself to immemorial human attitudes which we
> recognize by instinct as universal and true. I had not been
> mistaken. She was a battered woman now, not a lovely girl;
> but she still had that something which fires the imagination
> . . . She had only to stand in the orchard, to put her hand on
> a little crab tree and look up at the apples, to make you feel
> the goodness of planting and tending and harvesting.

In *My Antonia* the treatment of space is at first Edenic and Jim finds
consummation with the land in non-sexual terms. Later, at Antonia's
farm it becomes the maternal, procreative earth—the extension of the
feminine. Consequently in writing his book, Jim is united imaginatively
both with his muse and with the Nebraska landscape. He inserts the
possessive *My* into the title of his book because in writing the novel,
in reliving their shared experience, he possesses Antonia imaginatively
just as he comes to possess his earlier childhood self. But the novel
does not support Bob Kroetsch's argument that Lena Lingaard is the
muse that Jim fails to embrace. Lena is above all the epitome of the
compliant female. It is for this reason that both Antonia and Gaston
Cleric fear Jim's involvement with her. Presumably, if diverted by
Lena's "irresponsible" sexuality—or anybody else's for that matter—
Jim would not be able to write his epic of the West, his *Antonia*. Dante,
after all, had to be deprived of Beatrice. If anything, this is a view of
the creative process as sublimation rather than consummation.

      Similarly, Kroetsch's discussion of *As For Me and My House*
presents Philip as a failed novelist and Mrs. Bentley as the muse that
somehow fails to function. But the references to Philip as writer are
very minor in the novel—a few brief paragraphs at most. It is Philip as
artist that we hear most about and if we follow the increasing sureness
of his portrait, a sureness recorded by dispassionate observers, his is a
developing art. But I don't think that Mrs. Bentley is his muse, faulty
or otherwise. Initially Philip was inspired by the memory of his dead
father but by page 24 of the novel Judith West has taken over as muse:

> It's Judith tonight he's drawing. Or rather, trying to draw,
> for the strange swift whiteness of her face eludes him . . .
> He's out of himself, wrestling.

The important thing here is that Philip is finally "out of himself" and
this marks the beginning in his painting of a movement forward. After

meeting Judith, Philip stops painting false fronts and begins to confront authentic life. Presumably, Judith as muse is then fulfilling her function.

Even supposing we did want to develop the slight reference to Philip as failed novelist, Ross makes it clear that it is not Mrs. Bentley but Philip's own scrupulous artistry that makes his novel a commercial failure: "instead of trying to make his story popular and salable, he pushed it on somberly the way he felt it ought to go." Then too, the landscape portrayed in *As For Me and My House* appears to be without gender. It is equally fearful to men and women. Ross, like many Canadian writers, perceives an implacable landscape rather than Cather's beneficent garden.

> We've all lived in a little town too long. The wilderness makes us uneasy. I felt it first the night I walked alone along the river bank—a queer sense of something cold and fearful, something inanimate, yet aware of us.

I don't want to argue that Jim Burden is a sexually aggressive male; he isn't. Nor do I want to suggest that Mrs. Bentley is not a formidable figure; she is. But I am suggesting that the novels are more complex than the present sexist formula allows and that one of the clues to this complexity is to be found in their parallel structure.

Bob Kroetsch ends his paper with a series of questions. "What is the relationship between writer and written?" "Who is the protagonist in these novels," he wonders. "Is it Antonia or Jim Burden? Is it Philip Bentley or Mrs. Bentley?"

I would like to conclude my paper by responding to these questions. In the case of *As For Me and My House* we have Sinclair Ross writing about a woman who in her diary is writing about a man. The focus, therefore, is on the man, Philip, but it is on Philip in relation to his perceiver, Mrs. Bentley. In *My Antonia* we have Willa Cather writing about a man who has written an unpublished manuscript about a woman. The focus, therefore, is on the woman, Antonia, but in relation to her perceiver, Jim Burden. This narrative structure of using a figure of the opposite sex—a kind of transvestism—to comment on a character of one's own sex through an interior narrative is identical in both novels. This particular narrative structure seems to function as an adjustable focusing lens: on the one hand, it allows the author to distance himself from the subject; on the other hand, it allows the author to draw up specific images for close-up shots. It allows Cather to rhapsodize about Antonia and Ross to comment on Philip's relation with Mrs. Bentley without having these opinions reflected directly upon the author.

I see Cather and Ross psychologically linked with their protagonists Jim and Philip: both novels explore the problem of self-identity in relation to others. Sexual identity is, of course, a part of that larger issue. Cather with two books behind her had lost her dear friend, Isabel McClung, who had married. The following summer Cather returned to the prairies where she again met her childhood neighbour, Annie Pavelka, the immigrant girl who provided the model for Antonia. As the "neighbour" relationship suggests, it is Jim Burden who in the novel embodies some of Cather's characteristics: the evocation of Jim and Antonia in relationship becomes part of the exploration of Cather's childhood past.

Some twenty years after *My Antonia* Sinclair Ross was working in a bank in a Canadian prairie town where, incidentally, he, like his character, Philip, was invited to join the Church. Then in his early thirties he was writing short stories, wanting to be an artist, but still living with his mother who, as he says, "chattered on." In *As For Me and My House* there is a focusing on the artist, perhaps himself, who lives in a somewhat dependent relation to a beneficent as well as a constricting mother-wife. The resolution of this novel which has struck so many critics as aesthetically unsatisfactory seems to me to be quite appropriate psychologically. It is a true wish-fulfillment conclusion. Philip the artist is rescued by the muse, his true alter-ego, the pale, wincing Judith West and Mrs. Bentley, woman as mother and impediment to the artistic life is transformed into wife and helpmate.

I have enormous sympathy for the difficulties which men have in joining what Bob Kroetsch calls the "dance." But the evidence of these novels is that women too, have their difficulties. And for this "true testimony"—to vary a phrase which William Stafford used last night—we can only be grateful.

Canada and the Invention of the Western:
A Meditation on the Other Side of the Border

Leslie Fiedler

I shall be talking to you this afternoon not about the West, Canadian or American, but about the Western, in whose mythic world geographical or political boundaries are meaningless. I find it easier these days to deal with the latter than the former; as in a certain sense I always did, even during the twenty-three years I lived in Montana, becoming finally to myself a Montanan, but remaining always to my neighbors an out-lander, one whose sensibility had been made elsewhere. How could I tell those neighbors that my Eastern sensibility had been made in large part by Western novels, radio plays and movies, without betraying the fact that the physical West I shared with them remained for me always a little less *real* than the West of my childhood dreams.

Indeed, it seems even less real now that I return to it like any tourist from the East, having abandoned Missoula for the fleshpots of Buffalo some fourteen (it hardly seems possible!) years ago. I am told that when I finally left that state, which I had been invited to depart many times by old timers doubting my credentials and despising my politics, one of the last surviving Indian-fighting generals looked up from his bourbon and ditch and muttered, "I always knew that sonofa-bitch Fiedler would desert us in the end." And mythologically speaking, which you may gather is the way I prefer to speak, I guess I have.

But I have never deserted the Western and never will, as long as it remains available between hard covers or bound in paper or in comic book form or on radio or TV or whatever new medium is invented in what remains of the twentieth century to reach even larger audiences. Yet I used to be ashamed to admit my addiction to this essentially popular genre, precisely because it was available to everyone who could read either print on the page or images on the screen. And I resented that addiction in others who, it seemed to me, should have known better, like the cowboys who, coming into Missoula on free weekends, would head immediately for the sort of Western movie which I, stubbornly snobbish and elitist, had to believe falsified their actual lives.

I remained a snob and elitist, in fact, until I left the West for good, writing in one of the last essays I composed in that, *this* other world (the notes lie open before me as I transcribe this talk, and I cannot resist adding them as a kind of marginal commentary): "By and large, what we mean when we speak of 'the Western' is commodity literature, pulp entertainment, popular culture . . . the stuff of ten thousand films, TV scripts, magazine stories and cheap novels forgotten even as we experience them . . ." And I went on to deplore the fact that no "great epic" in prose or verse had been made, for instance, out of the adventures of Lewis and Clark, though Poe had once tried and, in his own way, Robert Penn Warren. Only more "cheap" fiction which I did not really forget, and, indeed, never shall.

What I should have known even then, what I *did* already know at some level of consciousness I could not touch, was that Epics are made not of history but of myth—more readily available in our age of Mass Culture to the popular writer and the popular audience than to the elite artist and the limited group of readers to whom he appeals. If we do have an Epic of the West, it is likely, I am trying to suggest, to be invisible to academic critics, who are looking for a work distinguished by lofty ideas and elegant form, both alien to the myth and fact of Western life.

Let me start again, then, for your benefit and mine, by defining the Western once more, this time without elitist presuppositions; though I believe that any valid discussion of literature and culture should move not from but toward definitions—at which, ideally, it never quite arrives. Only thus can it remain open rather than closed, suggestive rather than definitive: avoiding at all costs seeming to make a final statement rather than one more contribution to the continuing dialogue necessary to men and women who (like me) not only love reading stories, watching movies and TV, but, even more perhaps, talking about them.

I want to make it very clear, however, that my topic is not Western literature in general, i.e., all books written by writers who live in the West, or even all books set in that region; but rather all narrative, popular or elitist, printed, spoken, sung or translated into images on the screen—no matter where composed or by whom, and no matter what its setting—so long as it participates in, embodies, modifies or comments on the Myth of the West. By myth, I mean the kind of lie (fiction is a more honorific term) which tells a kind of truth unavailable to science, and unverifiable experimentally or statistically; an hallucination or fantasy or waking dream so widely shared that it alters for a nation, an ethnic group, a class, sometimes a large community cutting across all such lines, not just the perception of reality, but behaviour, which is to say, reality itself.

Like all myths, the Myth of the West tends to blur distinctions and boundaries important to academic literary critics, among them those which separate poetry from history, high art or belles lettres, from popular or junk culture, sometimes one national culture from another. Some myths, to be sure, are nationalist and particularist, reinforcing cultural separatism and chauvinism; but the Myth of the West is not. This may seem paradoxical at first glance, since that Myth is deeply associated from early on with America or perhaps rather the Americas; and after a while, with a specific period in American history and specific regions of the United States.

There is a real sense, indeed, in which, as I have argued in my book about Westerns, *The Return of the Vanishing American*, the Myth of the West *is* the Myth of America, and more particularly, of the making Americans: the transformation of White Europeans at the moment of confrontation with the New World Wilderness and its native Red inhabitants into something new—a new kind of human, different from both White and Red, as these had until that moment been traditionally, mythologically defined. But a little reflection will remind us that as soon as it was invented, the Myth of the West, like all myths, passed into the public domain: that region of waking dream which knows no linguistic or national boundaries.

"Hier oder Nirgends ist Amerika," here or nowhere is America, Goethe once said, realizing that one could, *must* find the mythological America wherever he happened to be, or nowhere at all. And similarly he might have said (I *do* say), "Here or nowhere is the West"—no matter where on the physical globe that "here" may be; for it exists really in our heads, in the altered consciousness not just of New Men in a New World, but of all men anywhere once that New World has been opened up to the imagination and those New Men have begun to celebrate themselves in song and story.

Small wonder then that mythographers of the West have come from everywhere in the world ever since, and that they continue to appear in what may seem at first the most unlikely places. One of the most successful and influential authors of popular Western novels in the nineteenth century, for instance, was Karl May, creator of Old

Shatterhand, a figure who haunted the minds of such latter-day Germans as Adolf Hitler, as well as writers whose books he banned and burned. And in the late twentieth century, Sergio Leone, whose native tongue and landscape are Italian, ranks high among makers of mythic Western films, more authentic archetypally than the movies the American Clint Eastwood has made on his own, since leaving Leone and trying to translate back into *his* native tongue and landscape the character created for him by the Italian director.

Similarly, the Japanese film maker Kurosawa, brought up, one presumes, on the images embodied in Tom Mix and the Lone Ranger, has managed to re-embody them in Samurai Warriors who remain somehow Western heroes all the same—as has been proved by the ease with which they can be re-translated into cowboys, merely by moving them back from Kyushu or Honshu to Arizona or Texas, where they began their mythic careers. Nor is geographical displacement necessary, if the director involved is an American such as Sam Peckinpah. Secure in his Amerindian blood and a long history of evoking machismo and violence on the Mexican he was able to make an English fiction like *Straw Dogs* into an unmistakeable Western without shifting its scene at all; and to convince us that a Jewish professor of mathematics from New York played by Dustin Hoffman was as adequate an avatar of the Westerner as any mythological plainsman acted by Gary Cooper.

Even easier was the mythological transformation of Jack Nicholson in *One Flew Over the Cuckoo's Nest*, whose Czech director seems scarcely to have known what he was doing, stripping Patrick MacMurphy not only of his red hair (the mere casting of Nicholson determined that), but even of the hob-nailed boots which connected him visibly with the lumbermen of the Rocky Mountain forests, yet leaving him still the Westerner: the Indian's friend, the enemy of White Woman.

It is not necessary that viewers of *Straw Dogs* and *One Flew Over the Cuckoo's Nest* recognize in such film narratives variations of the myth embodied also in the *Leatherstocking Tales, The Virginian, High Noon* and *Riders of the Purple Sage*, and invented before Zane Grey or Owen Wister or James Fenimore Cooper, by an old man, re-imagining what he had lived in fact in a world grown so remote from him that he could no longer recall it *as* fact. It is only necessary that they respond to it with appropriate passion and belief.

But the critic has another obligation: To make conscious what remains blessedly unconscious in others. And in this case, since I am the critic and Banff is the place in which I speak, to make us aware that the experiences and fantasies out of which that Myth of the West first arose join rather than separate our two cultures, having been half-lived, half-dreamed before the geographical boundaries, much less the hostilities and misunderstandings which now threaten to divide us from each other and our common heritage, had yet developed.

It emerged in what was still an undifferentiated New World wilderness, inhabited by as a still undifferentiated "us": a group of English-speaking refugees from the Old World, who explored that wilderness in fear and trembling and approached its alien original inhabitants in greed and violence, but somehow also in love. They were not yet settlers (settlement means the end of the West of the Western) this aboriginal " us," but strangers in a strange land, a place of wonder and magic, in which no traditional relationship or institution seemed viable, not marriage or the family, not state, school or church. Only war and, transcending it without eliminating it, a new kind of love. I return to the word "love" in due deliberation, because the Myth of the West which joins us to each other and the world is, as I have been insisting in print for some thirty years now, a myth of an unforeseen kind of love triumphing, perilously, temporarily, over the fear and hatred of an alien other.

Many years before I had discovered the classic American-Canadian text in which that love was first defined, I had already begun to suspect that however real the border between Canada and the United States might seem in the urban East, which I still inhabited, it scarcely existed on the mythological frontier to which I could escape merely by opening a book, switching on the radio or going to the movies. The first Western literature I ever encountered—and which has remained as real a part of my living past, a piece of my personal heritage, despite the fact that I was, am a third generation East European Jew raised in Newark, New Jersey—was the poetry of Robert Service.

Even before I had been introduced to the fiction of Max Brand and Zane Grey (much less Owen Wister or Cooper, who came to me in school rather than on the streets or at home), I already knew by heart large chunks of his poetry; since my father not only loved him and his verse, but considered it his duty to make me a real American by inducting me into the literature of what he, who never in his life actually escaped the urban East, thought of as the true, the essential, the authentic America: the West of the Westerns.

Even now, when I am drunk enough (though only these days when I am *that* drunk, since a long miseducation climaxing in a PhD in English Literature has taught me foolishly to despise such popular verse) I can recite most of "The Face on the Bar Room Floor." And in my deepest mythology, the mythology that binds me still to my childhood, my father and those friends who never made it to college, much less graduate school, Dan McGrew and Sam Magee live on beside Huckleberry Finn and Uncle Tom and Rip Van Winkle—constituting my mythological ties to a mythological America, where no blood relative of mine had yet set foot. This may explain in part, why it is so hard for me really to feel that Service is not an American at all, but a Canadian, laureate of another culture, another country, committed these days to establishing an identity different from our own, and claiming him, therefire as *theirs* rather than *ours.*

Hard as this may be, however, I find it even harder to understand Canadians, usually academics, who hasten to disown Service, though I still see stacks of his books on the shelves of airport bookstores from Ontario to Alberta, where I find myself occasionally stranded with enough time on my hands to observe how eagerly those books are read still by ordinary Canadians. And to thumb nostalgically through his pages, not merely insensitive to what my Canadian colleagues think of as his quite un-Canadian vulgarity (after all, he spent much time in the States and France), but relishing it; and remembering that the Western is always, at its most authentic vulgar, a challenge to notions of High Culture, particularly in its more Anglophile manifestations. Indeed, it occurs to me that it may be the cultural insecurity, the eagerness to seem at ease with European canons of gentility and High Art that have so long plagued Canadian intellectuals, which prevented the development in Canada of a real tradition of the popular Western.

Nonetheless, as I first learned reading Thoreau's *A Week on the Concord and Merrimack Rivers* in the early 1960s, the erotic myth, the archetypal eros involving interethnic male bonding, which I had identified as early as 1948 as being not only peculiarly Western, but specifically American was originally the invention—or at least was first formulated in the year 1800—by a citizen of a country which by that time had committed itself to a destiny and identity different from that of the United States. I am talking, of course, about the fur trapper Alexander Henry, who died in Quebec in the early nineteenth century, rich, happy and a Canadian.

When I first wrote my infamous little essay, "Come Back to the Raft Ag'in, Huck Honey," just after the end of World War II, I was thinking primarily of *Huckleberry Finn* and *Moby Dick*, which

no one, including me, then considered "Westerns" at all. To be sure,
I alluded, too, to the *Leatherstocking Tales*, generally recognized
as the prototype of that popular genre; but it was a clue to the eros
of America as a whole which I sought, rather than of the West in
particular. And that clue I was convinced I had found in the myth
of a sacred anti-marriage joining together two males, one a rebellious
White American and the other a non-White, Red, Black or Polynesian.
Not until I came upon Thoreau's *A Week on the Concord and Merrimack
Rivers*, that covert or crypto-Western, which I had until then ignored,
did I realize that what I had been describing was the Myth of the West,
which antedates that of America.

I rather disliked and distrusted Thoreau at that point in
my life, having found *Walden* a mean-spirited book, and its author a
hypocrite, who talked grandiloquently about the flight from civilization
while living close enough to home to get back each night for dinner;
as well as a despiser of his own body, who purported to be an imaginary
Indian, yet never smoked anything stronger than lily bulbs. It was,
however, tobacco, the Red Man's "medicine," which had helped certain
Englishmen expand their old European consciousness before English
settlement of the New World had properly begun—just as whiskey,
"the White Man's Milk," had contracted the consciousness of the
Indian. But Thoreau eschewed tobacco as he did sex, so that even in
his re-telling of the encounter between Alexander Henry and his Indian
companion, Wawatam, in *A Week on the Concord and Merrimack
Rivers*, there is no such passing back and forth of the pipe as we find
in *Huckleberry Finn, The Last of the Mohicans* and *Moby Dick*. Where
Henry's original account tells us that he and his aboriginal friend
hunted and feasted and smoked tobacco together, Thoreau substitutes
for the final sacramental act "making maple sugar": an improbable
symbol for male bonding, especially since only Indian women tapped
maple trees or boiled down the sap.

Yet, with whatever reservations, Thoreau does retell that
classic Canadian-American tale of love, inserting it into the entry for
Wednesday, in the midst of what begins as an essay on "Friendship"
and turns into a discussion of the need for a native American mythology
capable of sustaining a great American Epic. Such a mythology, he
tells us, was to be found not in the pretentious poems and ambitious
novels written by his own compatriots, but in Henry's chronicle of
what befell him in the years between the French and Indian Wars and
the outbreak of the American War for Independence, when he criss-
crossed the borders between Michigan and Canada, as unaware that he

had left one nation for another as any Indian then or now.

Henry, Thoreau observes, wrote with the "truth and modera-
tion worthy of the father of history . . . and does not defer too much
to literature." And yet, he insists, his *Adventures* "reads like the
argument to a great poem on the primitive state of the country and
its inhabitants." Indeed, Thoreau concludes "what is most interesting
and valuable in it is not material for . . . history . . . the annals of the
country . . . but the . . . *perennials*, which are ever without date,"
meaning by "*perennials*," it is clear, timeless archetypes, primordial
images, myths.

The only myth he actually specifies, however, is what we have
already identified as the Myth of the West: the Edenic Idyll shared by
Henry and Wawatam, a relationship "almost bare and leafless, yet not
blossomless nor fruitless . . ." Reimagining the scene of their first
encounter, Thoreau seems on the verge of beginning the great poem
he has predicted. "The stern, imperturbable warrior, after fasting,
solitude and mortification of the body, comes to the white man's
lodge, and affirms that he is the white brother who he saw in his
dream . . . If Wawatam would . . . take his bowl of human broth made
of the trader's fellow countrymen, he must first find a place of safety
for his Friend . . . ."

But the poetry cannot be sustained, any more than the
relationship so perilously established in the interstices between their
two cultures. After "a winter of undisturbed and happy intercourse,"
they part as they must; Wawatam vanishing into the wilderness like
a figure in a dream, and Henry returning to the settlements, the
restrictions and rewards of a civilization which precludes such "essentially heathenish" relationships, "free and irresponsible . . . ."

Thoreau was aware, as we also must be aware, lest by senti-
mentalizing it we falsify the Myth of the West, that the sublimated
"intercourse" it dreams involves not just fleeing the world of women
but stepping outside of history: ignoring the war between England
and France which had overflowed onto our continent in the eighteenth
century, as a result of the long struggle between Protestant and Catholic
for the hegemony of Europe, along with all the wars between nation
states which have succeeded—and the uneasy times of peace as well.
That Myth, I am suggesting, implies not just a flight from the institutionalized combat, but from the civil institutions for which, in theory
at least, they are fought: the Settlement, Home, Women and Children,
Romantic Love, Domesticity—finally, Christian Humanism itself;
which is to say, everything that Europeans had come by the eighteenth

century to call "Civilization." Friendship, Thoreau warns us, meaning by that term the wilderness eros, "is not so kind as it is imagined . . . but consists with a certain disregard for men and their erections, the Christian duties and humanities . . . ."

Ironically, the dream of the West as escape from culture, eternally renewed by the unending flight from schoolmarms, mothers, wives, pastors, sod-busters, cops and courts, law and order itself, has not as far as I am aware (but I am relatively ignorant on this score and may well be wrong) continued to move the imagination of eminent Canadian makers of fiction, as it has that of our own classic writers; perhaps because of the competing myth of the Shire, or the eternal vigilance of the RCMP, or the simple and disconcerting fact that we were there first and continue still to pre-empt the popular imagination north as well as south of the border. A Canadian friend has suggested to me recently that the Canadian Huckleberry Finn is—Huckleberry Finn! And who needs another.

But even on our side of the border, the Myth of the West has been embodied in no single great epic poem, as Thoreau had hoped it might be. Instead, it appears in innumerable lesser narratives: some straddling the line between High Art and what elitists dismiss as mere junk, like *Huckleberry Finn, Catcher in the Rye* and *One Flew Over the Cuckoo's Nest*; some clearly and joyously on the side of "trash," like the thousands of pulp stories, films and TV scripts in which Henry and Wawatam reappear in manifold disguises, that fool no one, ranging from the Lone Ranger and Tonto to Captain Kirk and Mr. Spock.

To be sure, we Americans have not—not most of us, most of the time at any rate, pledged as we are to the pursuit of security, success and domestic bliss—*lived* the Myth of the West. Even in the geographical West itself, we have, quite like Canadians, turned from pioneers, fur trappers, mountain men and cowpokes into sod-busters and city-dwellers; but for us the Myth of the West has never been converted into the myth of the gentleman farmer (despite the efforts of Thomas Jefferson) or the hardworking peasant (despite the fictions of transplanted but not transformed Europeans like O. E. Rolvaag).

We have, instead, continued—in the Pop tradition of the Western at least, which is, after all, the only tradition truly compatible with its anti-high cultural stance—to dream that we remain forever Strangers in a Strange Land, men without women or fixed abode, who even in the wilderness of cities are Midnight Cowboys still. And such a communal dream tells, as I began by suggesting, its own kind of truth, unique and incontrovertible. I am, therefore, moved to say of it in conclusion what Thoreau in *A Week* says of a very private dream of his own: "... in dreams we never deceive ourselves, nor are deceived ... In dreams we see ourselves naked and acting out our true characters ... Our truest life is when we are in dreams awake."

Response: **Canada and the Invention
of the Western:
*A Meditation on
the Other Side of the Border***

Jack Brenner

For over thirty years Leslie Fiedler has labored to lay bare that white
bone of myth he glimpsed at the bottom of our fondest fictions,
sending back to us, from time to time, field reports. If we have not
read those reports, or if we have read them grudgingly or meanly, put
off perhaps by what seemed either cocksureness or a deliberately wicked
stance, so much the worse for us. It can be claimed that *Love and
Death in the American Novel* is an indispensable book, not because
it settles all of the questions, but because it contains some of the most
revealing, suggestive and penetrating sentences anyone has ever written
about American literature. Each of us, probably, if we have read
Fiedler at all seriously, has had to back up, take stock, reassess, argue;
Fiedler, unlike so many other critics, makes a difference. For me, as
a Westerner concerned with both fiction and the West, *The Return of
the Vanishing American* is a crucial book, even though I'm impatient
with the weight Fiedler gave to what now seems trendy '60s psychedelia.
At any rate, Fiedler's essential service to us can't be challenged: by
discerning that deep, mythic shape of our fictions, he has been able
to tell us as much about ourselves as anyone now writing.

      If I then say that I find Fiedler's "Meditation" disappointing,
I want to be as clear as I can about why that's so. And I find the first,
obvious, reason for my disappointment and grumpiness close to hand:
I have heard it before. I don't mean that Fiedler should be obligated by
my own interest—that, since I have read his work with care and profit,
he must produce something new for me; I mean only that what he
says in the "Meditation" he has said before, and even in the same
language. The story of Alexander Henry and Wawatam, as retold by
Thoreau, is a bedrock point in *The Return of the Vanishing American*,
and transplanting it here gives the speech a weary, got-up-for-the-
occasion air. Moreover, I find my grumpiness fanned when Fiedler,

speaking from a position fixed, polished and comfortable with use, says that "any valid discussion of literature and culture should move not from but toward definitions—at which, ideally, it never quite arrives."

But all that, now I've written it, seems trivial and niggling, even a bit mean-spirited. How many ideas is a critic required to have? Fiedler has had a God's plenty, as anyone who reads his *Collected Essays* can see, and if the press of time and fame have led him over old ground on this occasion, so be it. Any teacher, required to perform publicly, knows how and why that can happen.

Even so, Fiedler's blue chips seem tarnished here, and for other reasons than simple use of older material. To show something of what I mean, I want to review what he says. We know, by now, what Fiedler means when he says he prefers to speak "mythologically" about the Western. If Karl May could write his stories about Old Shatterhand, if Italian and Japanese directors can make Western movies, then anyone can claim citizenship in that mythic territory in which geographical and political boundaries have no place. Fiedler can even point to his own experience as a latter-day re-enactment of the central mythic encounter between the European and the New World. "Hier oder Nirgends ist Amerika," Goethe said, and Fiedler shows how that has been true in his own life. Here or nowhere does America, or the West, exist, but in the mind of a third-generation urban Jew who lived for years in Montana and for whom the physical West is less real than his earliest dreams of the West.[1] And the core of that myth, that dream, carried to Fiedler through movies and classic American novels and radio programs, is the "sacred anti-marriage" between a rebellious white and another man of color, the male bond of non-sexual love that repudiates the civilization the white is both part of and fleeing, the bond which alters consciousness in both men. Alexander Henry and Wawatam, Queequeq and Ishmael, Huck and Jim, the Lone Ranger and Tonto, Chief Bromden and McMurphy—in those figures, Fiedler says, we see the classic Canadian-American tale of "an unforeseen kind of love triumphing, perilously, temporarily, over the fear and hatred of an alien other." It is not surprising to hear Fiedler speak of love here, since he has always been concerned with tracking down the eros energizing our fictions, but it *is* somewhat surprising to find Fiedler turning the myth to the uses of Canadian-American amity.

If Alexander Henry, the Canadian fur trapper, "invented" the Western myth before America was even a nation, Fiedler can claim "that the experiences and fantasies out of which that Myth of the West first arose join rather than separate our two cultures" and knowledge of this "common heritage" might lessen "the hostilities and misunder-standings which now threaten to divide us." But that myth, in Fiedler's words, implies "not just a flight from the institutionalized combat, but from the civil institutions for which, in theory at least, they are fought: the Settlement, Home, Women and Children, Romantic Love, Domesticity—finally Christian Humanism itself." So Canadians and Americans are joined, if I read Fiedler correctly, in the "communal dream" in which "we remain forever Strangers in a Strange Land, men without women or a fixed abode, who even in the wilderness of cities are Midnight Cowboys still."

That claim of mythic brotherhood seems, at best, forced. I'm uncomfortable with the easy use of "we" and "communal dream," for that "we" seems a truncated community: essentially, those men in flight from women and civilization. Perhaps Fiedler could say that he did not design the myth, and is only reporting a mythic truth, and that now we need to make use of whatever ties bind us. Yet the claim that men in retreat from women are brothers under the national skin, and that the brotherhood so formed can be a basis for solving present political difficulties, seems a strange idea indeed. If seriously meant, Fiedler's use of the myth appears to be as exclusionary of women as is the myth itself.

I am reminded, in thinking about Fiedler's apparent fall into what he once scornfully termed the Higher Masculine Sentimentality, of something Coleridge says in the *Biographia Literaria*. There Coleridge remembers a composition teacher who had a short way with pompous figures of speech: "Harp? Harp? Lyre? Pen and Ink, boy, you mean! Pierian Spring? Oh, aye! the cloister pump, I suppose!" This teacher's ire was roused especially by "similes and examples" used in a blanket way, particularly the story of Alexander and Clytus, "which was equally good and apt whatever might be the theme." "Was it ambition? Alexander and Clytus! Flattery? Alexander and Clytus! Anger? Drunk-enness? Pride? Friendship? Ingratitude? Late Repentance? Still, still Alexander and Clytus!" Finally, when one student praised agricultural life by observing that had Alexander been holding a plow, "he would not have run his friend Clytus through with a spear," the teacher banished Alexander and Clytus, "this servicable old friend," by public edict.

I mean to say, of course, that Fiedler's use of Alexander Henry and Wawatam makes the story begin to seem a servicable old friend that will do on almost any occasion. Friendship? Anger? *The* American Myth? Crossing Borders? Still, still Henry and Wawatam. This is not to say that the story has but one fixed meaning, or that it should be banished, but only that in this speech Fiedler seems to patch up old connections, tries to turn them another way, and somehow the energy to make them work is not there.

This quality of Fiedler's speech reflects a general characteristic of Fiedler's criticism, one that can be fine and exciting when it works. I'll try to show what I mean through this paragraph, which comes after Fiedler's claim that recognition of "our" common participation in the male myth could bring Canada and America closer:

> Ironically, the dream of the West as escape from culture, eternally renewed by the unending flight from schoolmarms, mothers, wives, pastors, sod-busters, cops and courts, law and order itself, has not as far as I am aware (but I am relatively ignorant on this score and may well be wrong) continued to move the imagination of eminent Canadian makers of fiction, as it has that of our own classic writers; perhaps because of the competing myth of the Shire, or the eternal vigilance of the RCMP, or the simple and disconcerting fact that we were there first and continue still to pre-empt the popular imagination north as well as south of the border. A Canadian friend has suggested to me recently that the Canadian Huckleberry Finn is—Huckleberry Finn! And who needs another?

One could be niggling about that statement, and observe that if the Myth of the West has not continued to engage the imaginations of Canadian writers, then the one instance upon which Fiedler builds his speech—Henry and Wawatam—might be a sport, a one-time-only, and therefore not so significant as Fiedler makes it, certainly not much evidence for male brotherhood that will bind up political wounds. But I am more interested in Fiedler's manner, his stance. Here we see Fiedler brushing aside the fact that Canadian fiction probably does not exhibit those concerns he has ascribed to it, the absence of a Huck Finn accounted for by a beginning "Ironically" and a final "And who needs another?". The stance might fairly be described as "imperial" —though I want to make clear that I am using the term in a fairly special sense.

Roger Sale, writing about a group of novelists he calls imperial (*Ploughshares* 4/3, 1978), gives me the terms. Sale's imperial novels seem so different as to resist any classification: *Catch-22, Why Are We in Vietnam?, V., Gravity's Rainbow, Portnoy's Complaint, Ragtime*, and many others. What ties these novels together, in spite of their differences and originalities, is the way in which, as Sale says, their "demeanor is individual and commanding: 'I call the shots here,' says the imperial novelist in every sentence, 'and I will not conceal for a minute who I am, though I have no intention of telling you anything more than I choose to.'" Sale goes on to say that "Underlying it all is a huge assertion of personal power, which leads to aggressive showmanship . . . in other words, style used as a badge of personal authority, and personal authority having the ability to invent and master whole worlds." So Sale's point in using the word "imperial" is "to suggest an analogy between these writers and their period, and to say that while most of these writers detest the American empire, they were in fact also expressing it, and deriving some of their enormous energy from it."

In using "imperial" to suggest some qualities of Fiedler's criticism, then, I want to leave the usual, closed-off political meaning of the word behind. In Fiedler's best criticism there has always been that sense of "I call the shots here," that assertion of personal authority over facts which could invent and master whole worlds, but sometimes leading (as in this speech or his essay on Hemingway's death) to feats of aggressive showmanship. And Fiedler's view of the West has always carried that struggle of repudiating the energy he saw there, even while he was charged by that energy. No one has told us more, in his sometimes imperial way, about masculine imperialism in conquest of the Alien Other. And no one else has insisted upon the West as an "authentically vulgar" corrective to gentility and elitism quite so eloquently, and sometimes so elegantly, as Fiedler has. There often is a certain swagger in this, a *chutzpah* that likes itself, so that Fiedler will claim to have been miseducated or will wonder if the trouble with Canadian intellectuals is that they are too genteel to read Service —but a *chutzpah*, I should quickly add, that Fiedler is aware of and owns readily. One of his finest pieces, to my mind, is an essay called "*Chutzpah* and *Pudeur*," and a few sentences from that will show concretely what I mean about the imperial impulse. He begins:

> If *chutzpah* and *pudeur* seem an ill-assorted pair of words, one of those mixed marriages (or unblessed acts of miscegenation) which everyone thinks should not and cannot last, but everyone knows most often do, this is because they are in fact such a mismatch; which is to say, made not in heaven but in the head of some perverse matchmaker, some misguided *shadchan*—in this case, me. I had never seen them consorting together on a printed page, the delicate French word, appropriate to a tradition of tact and learning, and the vulgar Yiddish one, so suitable to a countertradition in which arrogance and self-deprecating irony reinforce rather than cancel each other out . . . .

Not to have made the conjunction public, once it had occurred to me, would have been to betray a lack of gall, nerve, *chutzpah*, to put it precisely; but not to have regretted it a little almost immediately, would have been to reveal so total an absence of decorum that the very notion of boldness would have lost all meaning.

So Fiedler will make the marriage between the two ill-assorted terms, will perform these divided poles into a relation. And a fine marriage it is, with a splendid energy even in asides, an authentic interest in seeing where his energy can take him, a masterful, mastering performance.

More often than not, Fiedler's performances have been this exciting, challenging, even wonderful. But when criticism runs on swagger, inspiration, energy, what happens when the energy runs down? I think we can see the result in this speech. The old imperial gestures are there—"Watch me cross, or cross out, *these* borders"—but the energy is not. And perhaps the great danger of the imperial imagination is that what it most energetically asserts it will finally tame, so that any of us listening to Fiedler speak might justifiably say afterwards that he has grown weary in this West that once so sparked him, has made commonplace what was once wonderful.

Note

1   Since this basic idea of Fiedler's has sparked so much antagonism, particularly among Westerners, I want to offer some alternative terms. Wright Morris, who has produced a fine, rich body of fiction which is built precisely on the conviction that it is "fictions" which become our most significant "facts," has this to say in *The Territory Ahead*:

> Life, raw life, the kind we lead every day, whether it leads us into the past or the future, has the curious property of not seeming *real* enough. We have a need, however illusive, for a life that is more real than life. It lies in the imagination. Fiction would seem to be the way it is processed into reality. If this were not so we should have little excuse for art.

Substitute Fiedler's "myth" for Morris's "fiction" or "art" and the point is clear.

The Border League:
American "West"
and Canadian "Region"

Eli Mandel

Conferences, we are told, can cause a number of things to happen.
I note certain phrases in the "conference information" we received that
tell us what sorts of things might come to pass. "Crossing Frontiers"
will "bring together," suggest the "interchange of ideas across the lines
that separate," "encourage as much public and private discussion . . .
as possible," "provoke comparisons," "attempt assessments," "identify
promising areas," and in addition to all this, intrigue us with a "spouse's
program." Fair enough. My own attention must have been caught,
I think, by the peculiar resonance in the notion of crossing frontiers.
Long before this meeting, I had indeed written a paper on regionalism
in the Canadian novel which I entitled "Border-line Art" and while I
am not certain Marshall McLuhan knows of our proceedings I notice
that in an important new collection of essays entitled *The Canadian
Imagination* he has a piece entitled "Canada: the Border Line Case."[1]
Obviously, the metaphor of frontier and the actuality of border still
exercise a profound hold on the imagination of writers in this country.
It's difficult to see how it could be otherwise. I'll return to McLuhan's
paper in a moment because in his characteristically pell-mell way it
scatters insights about borders in Canada in all directions. It's impossible
not to be hit by one of them, if not entirely riddled by all. But I
begin by remarking on the obvious that the border between America
and Canada is of enormous importance in the imaginative life of any
Canadian, marking out, as it does, the interface of two major cultural
identities, historical definition, literary distinction. McLuhan takes his
epigraphs from Gertrude Stein about space in America: "In the United
States there is more space where nobody is than where anybody is.
This is what makes America what it is" and from Hugh Keenleyside,
"The boundary between Canada and the United States is a typically
human creation; it is physically invisible, geographically illogical,

militarily indefensible, and emotionally inescapable.[2] And so he marks out the two subjects I will concern myself with in talking about American and Canadian poetry of the West: space (Olson spells it with capital letters at the beginning of his exciting study of Melville); space, and borders. And I'll try to say where the borders bring our writers together and where they divide, how they mark out the spaces we occupy from those the American occupies, perhaps as in Earle Birney's witty capsule version of Canadian literary history:

> Can Lit
>
> since we'd always sky about
> when we had eagles they flew out
> leaving no shadow bigger than a wren's
> to trouble even our broodiest hens
>
> too busy bridging loneliness
> to be alone
> we hacked in railway ties
> what Emily etched in bone
>
> we French and English never lost
> our civil war
> endure it still
> a bloody civil bore
>
> the wounded sirened off
> no whitman wanted
> it's only by our lack of ghosts
> we're haunted

When I try to think of "West" in writing, I at once make a very odd set of personal connections: baseball, the Orpheum Theatre in Estevan, Saskatchewan, and Wallace Stegner's *Wolf Willow*. It's probably stretching things a bit to say they represent for me the three terms of the kind of discussion I want to carry on here but in fact I do think of them as the connections between literature, western mythology, and regionalism, the process of writing, the cowboy or wild west myth that I think of as American, and the regional definition that I think of as Canadian in writing of the West, especially in poetry.

Stegner's *Wolf Willow* exercises a profound attraction for me not only because of his interest in defining west as a region, not always an easy thing to do, but for two other reasons: (1) his sense of definition as mapping, and (2) the place that is west for him. Like the miniature or model worlds that entrance other regional writers, I think of James Reaney, Robert Kroetsch and Clark Blaise in particular, for Stegner, maps provide boundaries; and boundaries are not only areas of rich

interaction but of transformation too. His West, of Wolf Willow
(Whitemud he calls it, though its actual name, interestingly enough,
is Eastend), lies at the center of, or on the edge of, extraordinary
boundaries, the purpose of his book to trace those in their effects. Its
border lines are the line between the past and present, the line between
frontier culture and town culture, the line between north and south,
the watershed of the rivers running to the Arctic and those running
to the Gulf of Mexico, one of the great geographical and historical
divisions of North America, the line between the plains culture and
farm culture, between rancher and farmer, the ecological boundary of
glaciated and unglaciated land, and the surveyors' boundary, the forty-
ninth parallel; the book takes its definitions then in prehistory and
history, in legend, romance, and personal memory. Stegner's mapping
as well, I discovered to my delight, mapped out a place very like the
place I knew as a boy or rather more precisely, the place I didn't know
I knew, and its most profound boundary, as Stegner insists is that
between culture and nature, the distinction between a new land and
an old culture which Dick Harrison, in his important study of Canadian
Prairie Fiction *Unnamed Country*, occupies himself with in impressive
detail and clarity. Culturally, I was raised a Jewish Tennysonian in a
land which had little congruity either with my Russian immigrant
Shtetl family background or the twilight sensibility of a Victorian
poet. But not entirely escaping our American fate, the youngsters
with whom I grew in Estevan played out our young lives on the prairies
with metaphors of the West of Tom Mix and Buck Jones, heroes who
appear incongruously alongside imagery from Auschwitz in one of
my poems. I don't know which version of cowboy we were playing,
whether, to choose from three Eastern Canadian poets who have
given us their impressions, Atwood's, Smith's or Purdy's. Atwood's
and Purdy's I tend to discard now, since they are highly self-conscious
about their movie sources, as we certainly were not. In fact, in Atwood,
a backdrop addresses the cowboy figure sauntering out of the almost
silly West, on his face a porcelain grin, while he's tugging a papier-
mache cactus on wheels behind him with a string.[3] Purdy's is far more
the genuine movie myth except for the place it is being presented:

> The setting is really unreal
> about 150 Eskimos and whites
> jammed into a Nissen hut to
> watch Gary Cooper and Burt Lancaster
> in a technicolour western shootemup
> Eskimos don't understand the dialogue

at all but they like the action
and when noble Gary is in danger
or sinister Lancaster acts menacing
a tide of emotion sweeps the hot little hut
and kids crawling on the floor are quiet
sensing what their parents feel.4

As cultural comment, Purdy's poem is as impeccable as Atwood's, but
both I think have to be taken as criticism rather than symbol, not at
all part of the Western myth itself, simply because of the enormous
distance deliberately created between the myth and their own participation in it. I suppose in the end it is A. J. M. Smith's cowboy with whom
we would identify, though we would never have used his academic
language and precise imagery to describe the sensuality of the Western
myth, its sexual attractions that do not appear overtly again in Canadian
writing until Michael Ondaatje's *The Collected Works of Billy the Kid*
of which I'll say more later. Though in Smith's poem, a young girl
dreams her innocent sexual dream of gigantic cowboys, the same
blossoming must have occurred to us in those early border years:

Among the cigarettes and the peppermint creams
Came the flowers of fingers, luxurious and bland,
Incredibly blossoming in the little breast.
And in the Far West
The tremendous cowboys in goatskin pants
Shot up the town of her ignorant wish . . . .

In the holy name *bang! bang!* the flowers came
With the marvellous touch of fingers
Gentler than the fuzzy goats
Moving up and down, up and down as if in ecstasy
As the cowboys rode their skintight stallions
Over the barbarous hills of California.5

"These hidden borders in men's minds," says McLuhan, "are the great
vortices of energy and power that can spiral and erupt anywhere."6
Films of the border moved across the border and formed one of the
boundaries we will explore later. I knew the border in other ways,
through border towns like Portal and North Portal, for example, or
stories of bootlegging through the spaces between towns, and through
baseball. The Estevan Maple Leafs played in what was called the Border
League against towns like Noonan, Minot, Bismarck of North Dakota.
I never really thought of them as American teams, only better than
ours. A comment, I suppose, our ardent cultural nationalists would
seize upon as still another confession of a life under cultural imperialism.

And, of course, there were the momentous visits of the bearded House of David playing the all-black Kansas City Monarchs, strange heroes in a small Canadian town. The rule in Canada is that hockey defines our cultural identity, but like Edward McCourt in his prairie novels I think of the baseball tournament on a prairie sports day as a cultural definition. If Philip Roth is right in his *The Great American Novel*, baseball is the metaphor of American writing, politics and culture, a metaphoric leap rather difficult to make full sense of, but the Coover version in *The Universal Baseball Association, J. Henry Waugh Prop* points to other possibilities, the game as model or metaphor of writing itself. The regressiveness of the image of game inside game inside book is intriguing, as is a comment of John Cawelti's quoted by Dick Harrison to the effect that formulaic fiction assumes the important functions performed by game and ritual in older, cohesive cultures.[7] Here, a curious reversal occurs, game taking the part of formulaic fiction. In the terms I am working out here, the border, against whose presence I found myself formed, defined not only place as region but also a mythology of west, and the writing self, the deep dream of a people we are dreamed by in the intercourse of pen and paper, word and world.

It is, of course, one thing to work out the metaphoric implications of both "border" and "space" in America and Canada and to see both as forces common to the shaping of two cultures; it is quite another thing to observe in practice distinct literary modes of perceiving and manipulating those major metaphors and cultural definitions. McLuhan is right to observe as he does that in both Canadian and American writing new attitudes were developed to both inner and outer space, to spaces that had to be explored rather than inhabited, and that the immediate effect of continental space is to seem to be a land that has been explored but never lived in.[8] But if the "complex fate" of being a North American is worked out on the border line between aggression and hospitality, the dialectic of violence and civilization, it nonetheless remains that there appear characteristic differences between the Canadian and American response to those fateful conditions. In part, this paper proposes a preliminary sketch of what could be called a poetics of West, an attempt to say what in poetry distinguishes between Canadian and American West, if the terms are taken not so much as national as psychological in import. The difficulties are obvious, ranging as they do from the ambiguities of "West" to the inevitable theoretical puzzles of any kind of cultural history. Partly to skirt the difficulties, partly for convenience, I choose arbitrarily three writers to develop a schema of the differences between the contemporary Western in American poetry and contemporary regionalism in Canadian poetry: Edward Dorn's *Slinger*, Michael Ondaatje's *Collected Works of Billy the Kid*, and Robert Kroetsch's *Seed Catalogue*. Obviously, if I intended literary history the task would be more complicated and less symmetrical since it would, on the American side, move out to other kinds of West than Dorn's in the work, say, of Gary Snyder in *Myths and Texts*, McLure in his poetic dramas on Billy the Kid and Jean Harlow, Jack Spicer's *The Collected Books* and, on the Canadian side, to such poetics of space as in the spare elegant projectivism of Douglas Barbour, or in the desperate fantasy of John Newlove, or such narratives as the various Riel poems from William Hawkins's to Don Gutteridge's and a variety of west coast Westerns from the work of George Bowering to Roy Kyooka's *Fontainbleu Dream Machine*, and eastern Westerns of the variety most strikingly represented by a forgotten collection by Hawkins and McSkimming with one of the finest western titles ever conceived, *Shoot Low Sheriff, They're Riding Shetland Ponies*. As it is, there are difficulties enough even with the three I have chosen: Kroetsch, the Canadian regionalist, though born in Alberta has worked, studied and lived for most of his writing career in New York State; Ondaatje, whose *Billy the Kid* is an American Western, is an eastern Canadian born in Sri Lanka; and Dorn who is a westerner not by birth but by adoption, descends on his grandfather's side from a French-Canadian background; perhaps the three providing in themselves striking proof of McLuhan's thesis about border lines.

The distinction I propose is by no means new though I do not believe it has been developed in connection with contemporary poetry in any serious way. The theoretical foundation of discussions of the American West is impressively developed as is evident from the kinds of talent in many disciplines we have here at this conference and to whose speculations we owe so much and on which we must depend in our own arguments. Canadian regional theory of the West does not have anything of the same rigour or comprehensiveness, though in recent work by Laurie Ricou and, as I mentioned before, by Dick Harrison, distinct advances have been made while W. H. New's introduction to his essays *Articulating West* proposes a dialectic of a mythic West and civilized East which so far as I know has not been taken up with the seriousness it fully deserves. The development of regional poetry of the West in Canada is quite extraordinary and in its presence poses a number of yet unformulated challenges, though initial approaches have been made in such anthologies as Laurie Ricou's *Twelve Prairie Poets* and a large anthology of western Canadian poetry entitled *Number One Northern*.

At the outset of his study of Canadian prairie fiction, *Vertical Man/Horizontal World*, Laurie Ricou speaks of "the regional form of a question legitimately asked of all Canadian literature," the relation between writing and landscape, specifically, for his purposes, between the prairie and prairie writing.[9] A more extended and possibly more valuable form of the question is the one suggested by James K. Folsom in *The American Western Novel*:

> It is at least logically possible [he suggests] to distinguish two distinct methods for fictional treatment of Western themes. The first of these, most successfully pioneered by James Fenimore Cooper, is one . . . in [which] the author focuses his attention primarily upon a frontiersman and upon his reaction to the wild, uncivilized environment of the Great West. Such a novel chronicles man's impact upon the frontier, paying relatively little heed to the civilization which must follow on the frontiersman's heels. The second method . . . is the converse of this: in it the author focuses his attention primarily upon a given area of land, which he then watches develop from the pioneer state through various stages of civilization which follow.[10]

The distinction could be put as the one between a spiritual quest and an ancestral dream. Consider the quest which Olson so memorably describes in *Call Me Ishmael*, surely the point where any discussion of the American Western must now begin:

> I take SPACE to be the central fact to man born in America, from Folsom cave to now. I spell it large because it comes large here. Large and without mercy.
>
> It is geography at bottom, a hell of a wide land from the beginning. That made the first American story (Parkman's): exploration.
>
> Something else than a stretch of earth—seas on both sides, no barrier to contain as restless a thing as Western man was becoming in Columbus' day. That made Melville's story (part of it).
>
> PLUS a harshness we still perpetuate, a sun like a tomahawk, small earthquakes but big tornadoes and hurrikans, a river north and south in the middle of a land running out the blood.
>
> The fulcrum of America is the Plains, half sea half land, a high sun as metal and obdurate as the iron horizon, and a man's job is to sqare the circle.
>
> Some men ride on such space, others have to fasten themselves like a tent stake to survive. As I see it Poe dug in and Melville mounted. They are the alternatives.[11]

The rider and the stake under the hot sum, the metal land, the fulcrum
of America. Digging in or mounting and riding the whirlwind. "The
will to overwhelm nature that lies at the bottom of us" or the "will to
survive" the terror. These are the quite terrible choices Olson gives his
writers, and they have, in our time (his time) taken what is there to
be done. The Western as the space journey, journey through space, all
space, cosmic space, inner space, head space, by a spaced-out man. We
begin to approach the *Slinger*, Dorn's Western poem, by way of Olson,
which is as it should be.

      Connected so with space and place, the geographical question
as only Olson puts it, the Western transcends its merely formulaic and
ritualistic powers to claim for itself the central and most cogent poetics
of contemporary poetry. To say so much asks at least for some tempered
and considered comment, and for this reason more than any other
I take the liberty of quoting at some length from Donald Davie's
measured account of Olson and Dorn.

      It is place as a moving point, not as a fixed point that interests
Davie in the poetics of Olson and Dorn. Olson did not choose to
"concentrate on Gloucester simply because it happened to be the
poet's home town, out of some familiar Romantic notion of mystical
properties available for a man in his native origin, his 'roots' . . . He
chose to make Gloucester his standpoint, there was no mystical com-
pulsion on him to do so."[12] Thinking then of Olson's book on Melville,
Davie adds, "The standpoint which Olson, and more consistently Dorn,
are concerned to investigate is not characteristically a fixed point, the
place where roots are sunk; it is a moving point, the continually changing
standpoint of a man who is on the move across continents and oceans.
. . . Dorn's poem "Idaho Out" *gives us* this man moving . . . his standpoint changing as he moves, yet conditioned by the terrain it moves
through and over, as much as by the consciousness which occupies the
moving point."[13] The argument itself then moves to the significance
of moving on: "The history of the Western States—both the brief
recorded history, and the much longer unrecorded history of the
indigenous Indian peoples—is a history of human *movement*; and the
still largely empty landscape of those territories are images of nomadic
life to which the imaginative response is still (as it always has been)
to *move*, to *keep moving*. Moreover, because the human history of
those territories is so short and scant, and because they are still so
empty, the spectacle of them—like the spectacle of the oceans when
one travels on them—teases the imagination into conceiving that human
migrations across these spaces are only the last chapter of a history of

non-human migrations, a history which is read out of geology and climatology."14

But Dorn discerned a more spectacular possibility of the encounter with space and movement. After his collection entitled *Geography*, Dorn published *The North Atlantic Turbine*, about another interface of energy and vortices, but, as Davie tells us, he announced he wanted this collection "to be the last necessity to work out such locations," his interest now taken by the possibilities that constitute *Slinger*: "That non-spatial dimension, intensity, is one of the few singular things which interest me now."15

How to deploy the story of the journey through place, the moving point, to the ends of non-spatial intensity is only one of the major paradoxical questions of *Slinger*:16

> Time [Slinger says at the beginning of the poem],
> Time is more fundamental than space.
> It is, indeed, the most pervasive
> of all the categories
> in other words
> theres plenty of it.
> And it stretches things themselves
> until they blend into one,
> so if youve seen one thing
> youve seen them all.

It was William Carlos Williams, after all, who said, "a new world is only a new mind." And so too identity loses its significance as individuation: a kind of group brain, the characters of the poem, constitute a single identity to whom the poem occurs. Slinger, the gunman who has lived more than 2,000 years, seeks out Lil, the madam who he knew in Smyrna, meets the pronominally named character I, the poet bard called simply Poet, a wanderer named Kool Everything, and of course moves with his quite wonderful horse, the most philosophic, pedantic, linguistically alert of the whole group, continually stoned, as one might expect, on grass. I and Everything, partly because of their names, are sources of endless syntactical jokes and so a major clue to the method of the poem. The doctrine of Parmenides, *nothing changes*, arrives in a night letter in Book Three delivered from the Secretary to Parmenides by the goggled pilot of a biplane in the midst of some of the high science-fiction hilarity of the later parts of the poem. The Parmenidean doctrine is embodied throughout in the deconstruction of space, time, and identity made possible through syntactical derangement, puns, jokes, impossibilities. As a form of linguistic analysis, the poem adapts the Western story to the metaphor of a space poem in the spaced-out jargon of an acid and cocaine culture and in the language of Kool Everything.

But it is no more possible to describe the mental landscape of the poem than to do justice to the psychological and cosmic landscape of a Blakean prophecy to which *Slinger* bears more than a passing resemblance. The occasions of the poem are wildly surrealistic, comically philosophical or metaphysical. They range through a variety of trips, conversations, dialogues, recitals, incidental shootings, and slapstick anatomical distortions frequently the subject of extended debate. At request, the poet sings variously the Song of the woman, the raga "The Coast of the Firmament," a series of variations of the line "Cool Liquid Comes," recites "the Cycle of the Enchanted Wallet of Robarts, the Valfather of this Race," and celebrates in song the powers of Co-Kang. Supporting characters appear and disappear disconcertingly, notably Dr. Flamboyant in his Turing Machine, only partially manifested from Beenville, another time, the Speaking Barrel who debates the meaning of a finger in the ear of Kool Everything, and toward the conclusion a new group which includes La Bella Donna, Tonto Pronto from Toronto, Taco DeSoxin, and the mysteriously threatening unspecified gangs of Sllabs and Mogollones. And since time itself has become stretched in the one moment, a structure of literary allusion allows for all poems in the one, marvellously lyric evocations of past time and setting, the Prolegomenon to Book IIII, for example, recalling Jonson's masques and songs, Book III introduced by a learned and lovely Donne-like invocation of winter and daylight.

The space of *Slinger* is linguistic and perceptual, the border, as the motto for Book III tells us, is the line between the inside real and the outside real, between psychological and cosmic space crossed in the moment of perception in the language field. If there can be any summary, it is in Slinger's farewell to his friends:

> Many the wonders this day I have seen . . .
> Keen, fitful gusts are whispering here and there
> The mesas quiver above the withdrawing sunne
> Among the bushes half leafless and dry
> The smallest things now have their time
> The stars look very cold about the sky
> And I have grown to love your local star
> But now, ninos, it is time for me to go inside
> I must catch the timetrain

> The parabolas are in sympathy
> But it grieves me in some slight way
> because this has been such a fine play
> and I'll miss this marvellous accidentalism

The possibilities of the Western as a means of exploring perceptual reality occupy Michael Ondaatje too in his *The Collected Works of Billy the Kid*. Here the syntax is filmic, the field of action or border space the human body itself. Ondaatje moves easily, lyrically, and explosively in an area he calls border blur, taking the term from the concrete poet, B. P. Nichol, who also wrote a Billy the Kid poem and who forms the subject of Ondaatje's film, *Sons of Captain Poetry*. Border Blur refers to the mixed genre form of *Billy the Kid*, its quite extraordinary mixture of documentary, photographs, ballads, prose poems, lyrics as a means of developing the narrative of Billy's final encounter with Pat Garret. The mix allows for the film treatment Ondaatje intended through opening up new syntactical possibilities: cross-cutting, foreshortening, montage, dissolves, altered perspectives, close-ups.

In an interview with Sam Solecki, Ondaatje comments on his interest in film in answer to a question as to why Leone's *Once Upon a Time in the West* is one of his favourite movies:

> I'm not quite sure there's an intellectual reason, but emotionally I like that film's expansiveness and I find it a very moving film in the way it deals with the destruction of social violence by the violence of outsiders—something that interests me. And, ah, well I don't really like to intellectualize that film; it is delightful. It also contains the whole history of the western: there's a scene where just before the family is shot all the birds fly off which Leone has literally taken from Ford's *The Searchers*; the shooting through the boot is from a Gene Autry film and so on. I don't know how Leone gets away with it without seeming too self conscious but he does. Luckily I saw the film after I had finished *Billy the Kid* because here was an Italian film-maker making this western, in many ways the best western, where with *Billy the Kid* I was trying to make the film I couldn't afford to shoot, in the form of a book. All those B movies in which strange things didn't happen but could and should have happened I explored in the book.17

The comment not only locates Ondaatje's Western in its formal tradition but thematically as well. The immediacy of film effects Ondaatje connects rightly with the perceptual problem that interests him, the narrative circling its target like a crazed camera wheeling back on the image it has attempted to locate. Elsewhere I've commented on what I call Ondaatje's physiological imagination, his tendency to bring together images of sexuality, dismemberment, and poetics, poetic and sexual obsession that lead to what Northrop Frye calls the anatomy as encyclopaedic form. In *Billy the Kid* the mythic endlessly repeated act of dismemberment occurs at the border line, the interface of body and world, as in the superbly realized lyric:

> moving across the world on horses
> body split at the edge of their necks
> neck sweat eating at my jeans
> moving across the world on horses
> so if I had a newsman's brain I'd say
> well some morals are physical
> must be clear and open
> like diagram of watch or star
> one must eliminate much
> that is one turns when the bullet leaves you
> walk off see none of the thrashing
> the very eyes welling up like bad drains
> believing then the moral of newspapers or gun
> where bodies are mindless as paper flowers you dont feed
> or give to drink
> that is why I can watch the stomachs of clocks
> shift their wheels and pins into each other
> and emerge living, for hours[18]

Balanced between sanity and insanity, between human machines and mechanical men, between the gentle hunter and neutral assassin, between the dialectic of violence that is form and energy, the poem seeks an impossible stasis at the furthest edge of being.

The poem has been read in a variety of ways, most strikingly, by Stephen Scobie, as an allegory of the artist as outlaw[19] and as the documentary of a contemporary post-modern sensibility for whom the only subject is the process that informs everything that lives, "precisely this interplay between lethally-alive earth and lethally-machined world."[20] Ondaatje's fascination with "the edge of things" is then as crucial to the sensibility that informs *Billy the Kid* as the obsession with violence and its anatomy.

"Why do I love most / among my heroes" he asks in a poem called "White Dwarves" "those / who sail to that perfect edge / where there is no social fuel?" And in *Billy the Kid*, against what has been called "delight in the precision of diagram or machine" is added "fascination with their hairspring balance at the very edge of breakdown":[21]

> The beautiful machines pivoting on themselves
> sealing and fusing to others
> and men throwing levers like coins at them.
> And there is the same stress as with stars
> the one altered move that will make them maniac.

The sense in which I have taken Dorn and Ondaatje as American writers is not so much a matter of their sensibility as their poetic strategies: in choosing western forms for their poems, they chose space, in Olson's sense, as their subject, though admittedly there appear to be some unsatisfactory contradictions involved, particularly in the way in which both contract space in their Westerns, Dorn to a non-spatial dimension of intensity, Ondaatje to points of stasis at the far edge of being. One could, I suppose, speak of them as, in the contemporary sense, far-out poets, though why that is singularly American is not easy to see at once, unless we are prepared to take the so-called post-modern assault on its own forms as particularly American. Another difficulty appears here, unfortunately. The third writer I want to consider, the one I have chosen as an example of Canadian regionalist, happens to be an editor of *Boundary 2*, a journal, as it calls itself, of post-modern writing. That puts Robert Kroetsch in the American camp where because of his situation as teacher and editor he certainly is for a very large part of his time. But whether by synchronicity, symmetry or just plain good luck, he happens as well to be a man who thrives on paradoxes, in his fiction, his poetry and his theorizing about literature, and so he points quickly to some possible ways out of the dilemma here.

     The most important is, I think, his own sense of place and West as a region of poetry which though it rises from American models quickly defines itself in peculiarly Canadian terms. This is the kind of paradox he loves: becoming Canadian by being American, he plays off differences between the two sensibilities; a self-consciously exiled writer in New York State writing in solitude broken by what he calls "cultural binges,"[22] hell-raising in whore houses, beer places, book stores and libraries, he defines himself in small-town terms from the midst of a center of cosmopolitan and international connections. The tensions are satisfying to what he takes as the Canadian as opposed to the American sensibility: Jungian rather than Freudian, dialectical rather than individualistic, communal not private, anti-historical rather than historical, the invisible face and missing voice of McLuhan's North American putting on the artist's mask and taking on the tribal voice at the borders of small towns where double plots play out magical transformations.

If Olson lies somewhere behind Dorn and Ondaatje, Williams is the one to seek in Kroetsch's *Ledger* and *Seed Catalogue*, or so Kroetsch puts it himself, not without some slyness, I think.

Asked in an interview, "Is Williams not an alien model for the prairie poet?" Kroetsch replies:

> It depends. You don't imitate, in a sense you emulate. You take the lesson rather than the actual poem. Look at his beginning of *Paterson* with the three words "a local pride." A Local pride is where you've got to begin, and we didn't have a local pride. Because all the models were telling us we didn't even exist. And that's what I take from Williams—the lesson of a beginning of a local pride.23

But if the regional Canadian poem begins in America, the regional *Western* Canadian poem, Kroetsch goes on to suggest, begins in the East:

> People doing it in the East, like Al Purdy, I'm sure were pretty important in the development of Prairie poetry. In abandoning given verse forms for the colloquial, the prosaic, telling yarns in the oral tradition.24

The anecdotal as opposed to the syntactical, poetry as story not as form, and as prose; not the line but the paragraph, not the margin but the whole page, not grammar but the list, not style but voice, and especially as Kroetsch says elsewhere, "a dream of origins," not real places but remembered places, "a dreamed condition, a remembered condition, an explanation of where we come from, a myth."25 The terms recall the dreamed impossible return of Suknaski's *Wood Mountain Poems*.

If Olson is right and Space is the central fact to man born in America, Kroetsch is right to locate the central concern born to a man in Canada to be the regional myth of origins. It is this concern in *Seed Catalogue*, I believe, articulated as it is, that makes the poem take its place alongside James Reaney's *Twelve Letters to a Small Town* and Atwood's *Journals of Susanna Moodie* as one of the three or four

indispensable and essential Canadian poems, and certainly as the central
poem of the Canadian West. Like the others I have mentioned, it is a
poem of definitions: it is a poem about itself as a poem, being a poem
in a place. As its own model, it defines itself in the way that Reaney's
Letters does as it seeks out the metaphors that will form the town
the poem is forming. The stunning paradox in *Seed Catalogue* is the
play on everything implied by *creation ex nihilo*. Structured simply
on the garden, gardener, seed catalogue metaphor, the poem in ten
parts develops the implications of the inevitable variations: How do
you grow a garden? How do you grow a gardener? How do you grow
a lover? How do you grow a prairie town? How do you grow a Past?
How do you grow a poet? It is a building, growing, creating poem:
out of the terror, out of the losses, out of the shards and fragments
of lives, their letters, documents, memories, speech, stories, big stories
and little stories, invocations and epilogues, first and last words, loves
and deaths, emptiness, all that the prairie wasn't, could not be, its
absences, emptiness and fulfilment, the plenitude of being. Seeds and
catalogues, the books we read. The prairie emerges precisely out of
its absences.

> How do you Grow a Poet?
> > Son, this is a crowbar.
> > This is a willow fencepost.
> > This is a sledge.
> > This is a roll of barbed wire.
> > This is a bag of staples.
> > This is a claw hammer.
> We give form to this land by running
> a series of posts and three strands
> of barbed wire around a 1/4 section.
> > First off I want you to take that
> > crowbar and drive 1,156 holes
> > in that gumbo.
> > And the next time you want to
> > write a poem
> > we'll start the haying.26
>
> How do you grow a garden?
> > No trees
> > around the house,
> > only the wind.
> > Only the January snow.
> > Only the summer sun.27

Some men ride on such space, others have to fasten themselves like a tent to a stake to survive. Some have ridden the whirlwind. Others have survived. What matters is that, however it was done, where there was emptiness, there are now words; where there was nothing, there are poems. Some dug in. Some mounted. Those have been the alternatives.

Notes

1   Marshall McLuhan, "Canada: The Border Line Case," *The Canadian Imagination*, ed. David Staines (Cambridge: Harvard University Press, 1977), pp. 226-248.

2   McLuhan, p. 226.

3   Margaret Atwood, "Backdrop Addresses Cowboy," *The Animals in that Country* (Oxford: Oxford University Press, 1968), pp. 50-51.

4   Al Purdy, "At the Movies," *North of Summer* (Toronto: McClelland and Stewart, 1967), p. 77.

5   A. J. M. Smith, "Far West," *Collected Poems* (Oxford: Oxford University Press, 1962), p. 58. Revised from *Book of Canadian Poetry*, 1957.

6   McLuhan, p. 241.

7   Dick Harrison, *Unnamed Country: The Struggle for a Canadian Prairie Fiction* (Edmonton: University of Alberta Press, 1977), p. 157.

8   McLuhan, p. 231.

9   Laurie Ricou, *Vertical Man/Horizontal World* (Vancouver: University of British Columbia Press, 1973), p. 2.

10 James K. Folsom, *The American Western Novel* (New Haven: College and University Press, 1966), p. 177.

11 Charles Olson, *Call Me Ishmael* (San Francisco: City Lights Books, 1947), pp. 11-12.

12 Donald Davie, "The Black Mountain Poets," *The Poet in the Imaginary Museum*, ed. Barry Alpert (Manchester: Carnacat, 1977), p. 182.

13 Davie, pp. 182-183.

14 Davie, p. 183.

15 Davie, p. 184.

16 Edward Dorn, *Slinger* (Wingbow Press, 1975), n.p.

17 Sam Solecki, "Interview with Michael Ondaatje," *Rune*, 2 (Spring 1975), 46.

18 Michael Ondaatje, *The Collected Works of Billy the Kid* (Toronto: Anansi, 1970), p. 11.

19 Stephen Scobie, "Two Authors in Search of a Character," *Canadian Literature*, 54 (Autumn 1972), 37-55.

20 Dennis Lee, *Savage Fields* (Toronto: Anansi, 1977), p. 21.

21 Lee, p. 20.

22 "Uncovering Our Dream World: An Interview with Robert Kroetsch," *Arts Manitoba*, 1:1 (Jan.-Feb. 1977), 32.

23 "Uncovering Our Dream World," p. 36.

24 "Uncovering Our Dream World," p. 36.

25 "Uncovering Our Dream World," p. 36.

26 Robert Kroetsch, *Seed Catalogue* (Winnipeg: Turnstone Press, 1977), p. 31.

27 Kroetsch, p. 47.

Response: The Border League: American "West" and Canadian "Region"

W. H. New

I have in my possession a photograph of Eli Mandel taken in a bird sanctuary in southern India. The day is bright; the sky is blue; the trees are calm; and Eli is standing, smiling, beside a signpost which reads: "Look out for crocodiles." I was reminded of this sign when I read the paper I have been asked to comment upon today. It smiles benignly, but it has teeth. And I am cast in the unenviable role of the bird that clambers around cleaning inside the crocodile's dental territory.

The fact that the sign is ambiguous—it was not intentionally a warning (*Look Out* for crocodiles) but rather a directional indicator (to the *Lookout*, for Crocodiles)—only intensifies the parallel, for what Eli has isolated for us today, commenting on notions of *space* and *boundary*, are the terrible ambiguities of location through which artists identify the kinetic worlds of their own imagination. Now . . . people are accustomed to seeing. Observing the world, they find in it things they recognize and things they find unfamiliar. But they attempt to make sense of both by interpreting them against a backdrop of their own experience. The indeterminacy of this process raises several immediate questions, like these: to what degree is perception daily distorted by misapprehensions great and small, by the cultural translation through which our minds record and arrange the data that experience provides? What is the nature of the multiple relationship between sociology and culture? Which precedes the other, or do the two grow simultaneously? What is the boundary line between accurate and inaccurate perception, and does this matter? Is it the same from person to person, and does *that* matter? Can one distinguish between a cast of mind that defines external boundaries in order to enfranchise internal space, and one that regulates internal attitudes in the assumption that freedom is located in external space? Are boundaries any different from edges? Is space any different from distance? How do culture and individuality both affect language? How does one *articulate* perceptions, perceiving, and the separate prospects of American space and Canadian region? And thus we are taken back into today's paper.

But I want to go back indirectly, by reading to you from one of my favorite essays by James Thurber, which contributes, I think, in its own way, to a discussion of place and voice and attitude of mind. The essay is called "The French Far West,"[1] and Thurber opens it by quoting one of E. M. Forster's observations about film: "'American women shoot the hippopotamus with eyebrows made of platinum.' I have given that remarkable sentence a great deal of study," Thurber adds,

> but I still do not know whether Mr. Forster means that American women have platinum eyebrows or that the hippopotamus has platinum eyebrows or that American women shoot platinum eyebrows into the hippopotamus. At any rate, it faintly stirred in my mind a dim train of elusive memories which were brightened up suddenly and brought into sharp focus for me when, one night, I went to see *The Plainsman*, a hard-riding, fast-shooting movie dealing with warfare in the Far West back in the bloody seventies. I knew then what Mr. Forster's curious and tantalizing sentence reminded me of. It was like nothing in the world so much as certain sentences which appeared in a group of French paperback dime (or, rather, twenty-five-centime) novels that I collected a dozen years ago in France. *The Plainsman* brought up these old pulp thrillers in all clarity for me because, like that movie, they dealt mainly with the stupendous activities of Buffalo Bill and Wild Bill Hickock; but in them were a unique fantasy, a special inventiveness, and an imaginative abandon beside which the movie treatment of the two heroes pales, as the saying goes, into nothing.

He goes on to recount his enthusiasm for one of the more "inspired" of these paperback books that he found in a stall along the Seine: *Les Aventures du Wild Bill dans le Far-Ouest*:

> Wild Bill Hickock was, in this wonderful and beautiful tale, an even more prodigious manipulator of the six-gun than he seems to have been in real life, which, as you must know, is saying a great deal. He frequently mowed down a hundred or two hundred Indians in a few minutes with his redoutable pistol. The French author of this masterpiece for some mysterious but delightful reason referred to Hickock sometimes as Wild

Bill and sometimes as Wild Bird. *'Bonjour, Wild Bill!'* his friend Buffalo Bill often said to him when they met, only to shout a moment later, *'Regardez, Wild Bird! Les Peaux-Rouges!'* The two heroes spent a great deal of their time, as in *The Plainsman*, helping each other out of dreadful situations. Once, for example, while hunting Seminoles in Florida, Buffalo Bill fell into a tiger trap that had been set for him by the Indians—he stepped onto what turned out to be sticks covered with grass, and plunged to the bottom of a deep pit. At this point our author wrote, *'"Mercy me!" s'ecria Buffalo Bill.'* The great scout was rescued, of course, by none other than Wild Bill, or Bird, who, emerging from the forest to see his old comrade in distress, could only exclaim, *'My word!'*

It was, I believe, in another volume that one of the most interesting characters in all French fiction of the Far West appeared, a certain Major Preston, alias Preeton, alias Preslon (the paperbacks rarely spelled anyone's name twice in succession the same way). This hero, we were told when he was introduced, 'had distinguished himself in the Civil War by capturing Pittsburgh,' a feat which makes Lee's invasion of Pennsylvania seem mere child's play. Major Preeton (I always preferred that alias) had come out West to fight the Indians with cannon, since he believed it absurd that nobody had thought to blow them off the face of the earth with cannon before. How he made out with his artillery against the forest skulkers I have forgotten, but I have an indelible memory of a certain close escape that Buffalo Bill had in this same book. It seems that through an oversight, he had set out on a scouting trip without his dynamite—he also carried, by the way, cheroots and a flashlight—and hence, when he stumbled upon a huge band of redskins, he had to ride as fast as he could for the nearest fort. He made it just in time. 'Buffalo Bill,' ran the story, 'clattered across the drawbridge and into the fort just ahead of the Indians, who, unable to stop in time, plunged into the moat and were drowned.' It may have been in this same tale that Buffalo Bill was once so hard pressed that he had to send for Wild Bird to help him out. Usually, when one was in trouble, the other showed up by a kind of instinct, but this time Wild Bird was nowhere to be found. It was a long time, in fact, before his whereabouts were discovered. You will never guess where he was. He was 'taking the baths at Atlantic City under orders of his physician.' But he came riding across the country in one day to Buffalo Bill's side, and all was well. Major Preeton, it sticks in my mind, got bored with the service in the Western hotels and went 'back to Philadelphia' (Philadelphia appears to have been the capital city of the United States at this time). The Indians in all these tales—and this is probably what gave Major Preeton his great idea—were seldom seen as individuals or in pairs or small groups, but prowled about in well-ordered columns of squads. I recall, however, one drawing (the paperbacks were copiously illustrated) which showed two *Peaux-Rouges* leaping upon and captured a scout who had wandered too far from his draw-bridge one night. The picture presented one of the Indians as smilingly taunting his captive, and the caption read, '*Vous vous promenez tres tard ce soir, mon vieux!*' This remained my favourite line until I saw one night in Paris an old W. S. Hart movie called *Le Roi du Far-Ouest*, in which Hart, insulted by a drunken ruffian, turned upon him and said, in his grim, laconic way, '*Et puis, apres?*'

After several other examples of the "delightful confusion and inaccuracy which threaded these wondrous stories," Thurber goes on:

There were, in my lost and lamented collection, a hundred other fine things, which I have forgotten, but there is one that will forever remain with me. It occurred in a book in which, as I remember it, Billy the Kid, alias Billy the Boy, was the central figure. At any rate, two strangers had turned up in a small Western town and their actions had aroused the suspi-cions of a group of respectable citizens, who forthwith called on the sheriff to complain about the newcomers. The sheriff listened gravely for a while, got up and buckled on his gun belt, and said, '*Alors, je vais demander ses cartes d'identite!*' There are few things, in any literature, that have ever given me a greater thrill than coming across that line.

The writer's enormous stylistic skill gives these reflections their char-acteristic humor. Not the least among the devices Thurber employs derives directly from the incongruity of the French phrases: or more particularly, from the cultural disparity we recognize when transporting —or literally translating—the phrases out of their unfamiliar French context into their (to some degree, at least) familiar American one. The issue is not simply that of "delightful confusion and inaccuracy"; This is merely Thurber's rhetorical disguise. Nor is it one of calling serious attention to Hollywood's errors and stereotypes, as Eli Mandel has pointed out Atwood and Purdy do—and one might add Berton's *Hollywood's Canada* and other examples as well. Rather, it is a matter of calling attention to the difference between factual error and creative inaccuracy, which is one of the murky borderlands of art and one to which Eli's paper repeatedly turns.

Essential to emphasize here, then, is that the western myths of Canada and the USA, even in English, are usually cheerfully inaccurate, but that we recognize them as being factually in error only when we transport them outside their own context. Some years back, when more or less all American children were wearing Davy Crockett hats and singing about the wild frontier—and when a high proportion of Canadian children were doing the same thing—the CBC confronted the importation of culture by developing a native television imitation: transforming the fur traders Radisson and Groseilliers into Crocket-like culture heroes, in whom, however, few Canadian children placed any faith whatsoever. As Mordecai Richler has pointed out, we have kept borrowing American frontier heroes (and sometimes, as with Superman, even invented them for Americans first) when we needed the vicarious thrills that such adventure myths provided. (I was reminded of the power of the borrowing just recently, when I was walking through a room in which a television set was enacting a quiz program; the precise question that was being asked is not one I can exactly remember— it had to do with old movies and movie heroes—but the answer leaped immediately and unbidden to my mind: it was *Sergeant Preston of the Yukon*; the American contestant, in obvious desperation, after a long pause suggested *Monte the Mountie*, which, as you might guess, failed to satisfy the quizmaster but gave me great delight.) What I am saying is that for the most part—call it ironic distance, if you like, or cultural bias, or perhaps voice—we distinguished between the vicariousness of the borrowed experience and the realities (whether empirical or mythic, physiological or colloquial) of the worlds we daily inhabited.

And here I come, recognizing both the power and the limited validity of recalled personal experience as a basis for critical doctrine, to Eli's central distinction between mythic space and bordered region— which I suspect is less an empirical truth (though it is a compelling suggestion) than a matter of vantage point. And that what is "space" to one culture is "region" to another, and vice-versa. It is fairly easy to classify all those French Westerns as games of myth-playing; they lie outside both space and region, and become interesting at the point they are brought into contact with them. What is a little more problematic is *Thurber's* connection: is it simply that of the Sophisticated (Ohio) Easterner holding himself aloof from the Western's giant simplicities? or is it that of the American child grown up to the daily re-enactment of the Western's cops-robbers/cowboys-Indians/winners-losers dualities in American life? It is significant, I think, that Thurber attaches the inaccurate Western to Europe, for Europe since the War

of Independence seems always to have constituted "Other" or "Not Us"
in American life, and proved both fascinating and rejectable. By contrast, Canadians grew with at least two varieties of "Other": Europe for
one, America for the second, both again rejectable and fascinating. But
here we encounter directly that border/line condition: the Canadian
borrowing of the American Western, stereotypes and culture figures and
all, has been part of a conscious play with "the edge of things" and
the "Other" that lies somewhere beyond (that Ondaatje admires
an *Italian* Western strikes me as more than just subjective partiality);
the American *declaration* of the American Western cannot be this, or be
exactly this process, but must engage itself with the realities of an
actual American environment from which the Western has emerged,
and which in some degree it has articulated and shaped. Where does the
play end and the reality begin? or does the prevalent *game* metaphor
that articulates American politics mean that in American space—now
a galactic frontier and not just a Western one—reality has been so long
identified with play that the distinction between them is hard to
locate or perceive or admit? I know nothing about the work of Dorn,
to whom Eli Mandel has referred; but I am nonetheless struck by
the phrasing of one of the passages from *Slinger* that he read, and
I want to reiterate it now, for it seems to me to brood over this
differentiation:

> Many the wonders this day I have seen . . .
> Keen, fitful gusts are whispering here and there
> The mesas quiver above the withdrawing sunne
> Among the bushes half leafless and dry
> The smallest things now have their time
> The stars look very cold about the sky
> And I have grown to love your local star
> But now, ninos, it is time for me to go inside
> I must catch the timetrain
> The parabolas are in sympathy
> But it grieves me in some slight way
> because this has been such a fine play
> and I'll miss this marvellous accidentalism

What was a childlike imaginative revel in the realities of word resolves
itself in a dualistic confrontation between word and world, in which—
apparently—one side must surrender to the other.

For Robert Kroetsch, however—and as Eli rightly emphasized,
it is one of the particular accomplishments of Kroetsch's *Seed Catalogue*
—word and world appear to be one. In the Canadian West—that settle-

ment, as Dick Harrison and Lewis Thomas have usefully reminded us,[2] of Central Canada—the simple confrontations have proved over time to be inexact descriptions of people's relationship with region. There may be a growing lassitude there: an increased local adoption of inexact language and borrowed social structures. But for Kroetsch, whose interest is in home more than territory, in energy more than space, the imported distinction between the will to deny the land and the desire to be illuminated by the land (for *land*, read *wilderness*, read *unconscious*, read *imagination*) does not end up as an either/or distinction, and he strives repeatedly—through legend and fable and "symmetry" and "Border Blur"—to find a literary means that will sound the paradoxes of his society without becoming culturally reductive, and evoke the fluidity of his private vision without becoming technically abstruse. In *Seed Catalogue*, we are told as the preface to a last will and testament that "we silence words / by writing them down." We are told that there are dangers in "merely living" and "standing still," and that growing is hard. We are told that West is winter, and we know that it is only over distance that the seed catalogues arrive. But winter also contains the summer sun; we see all kinds of seed catalogues bloom; and we see "the home place" in constant process:

> Winter was ending.
> This is what happened:
> we were harrowing the garden.
> You've got to understand this:
> I was sitting on the horse.
> The horse was standing still.
> I fell off.

>> The hired man laughed: how
>> in hell did you manage to
>> fall off a horse that was
>> *standing still*?

>>> Bring me the radish seeds,
>>> my mother whispered.

> No trees
> around the house.
> Only the wind.
> Only the January snow.
> Only the summer sun.
> The home place:
> a terrible symmetry.

How do you grow a gardener?

> Telephone Peas
> Garden Gem Carrots
> Early Snowcap Cauliflower
> Perfection Globe Onions
> Hubbard Squash
> Early Ohio Potatoes

> This is what happened—at my mother's wake. This
> is a fact—the World Series was in progress. The
> Cincinnati Reds were playing the Detroit Tigers.
> It was raining. The road to the graveyard was barely
> passable. The horse was standing still. Bring me
> the radish seeds, my mother whispered.[3]

A way of living thus grows into a way of saying, waiting only for an aesthetic of voice and listeners with the ears to hear.

In a poem called "Historia Animalium" which appears later in *Seed Catalogue*, Kroetsch makes a further point. It acknowledges openly his ambivalent attitudes to form, and his determination— a predicament we can recognize and share—to commit himself none- theless to literary endeavor. There is a brief headnote, which reads: "When the crocodile yawns the trochilus flies into his mouth and cleans his teeth"—and then the poem goes on this way:

> There are no crocodiles in Saskatchewan
> to speak of.
> No victim's cries nor
> vermined stink of Nile.

> Yet does the glutted day but yawn
> and trochili we whiz
> into the tree-bare horizon:
> reckless to beak old pleasures
> from the undevoured flesh:

> risking the clamp of
> words.[4]

Notes

1   James Thurber, "Wild Bird Hickock and His Friends," in *Let Your Mind Alone* by Helen W. Thurber and Rosemary Thurber Sauers (New York: Harper and Row, 1965), pp. 115-118. Originally published in *The New Yorker*.

2   Dick Harrison, *Unnamed Country: The Struggle for a Canadian Prairie Fiction* (Edmonton: University of Alberta Press, 1977); and L. G. Thomas in his conference paper.

3   Robert Kroetsch, *Seed Catalogue* (Winnipeg: Turnstone Press, 1977), pp. 11, 13, 15.

4   Kroetsch, p. 58.

Summing Up

Richard Etulain

During the past three days I have been searching for suitable symbols to express my feelings about being here in Banff and taking part in this stimulating conference. Perhaps one appropriate reaction is that of the western explorers Meriwether Lewis and William Clark when in 1805 they first glimpsed the Pacific Ocean. Their enthusiastic "O Joy!" illustrates some of the emotion I feel in experiencing the initial conference devoted to the study of the literary Wests of Canada and the United States.

A second event that occurred a few decades after the explorers' discovery of the Pacific exemplifies another side of my reactions. Herman Melville, while reading for the first time a collection of short stories by Nathaniel Hawthorne, experienced what he termed a "shock of recognition." Possibly others sense with me the growing desire in Canada and the United States to examine the literary cultures of our western regions. As we hear and read of these efforts of students and scholars on each side of the border, we experience a moment of epiphany in the shared problems of studying and analyzing new cultures.

In reading through a limited number of essays and books about Canadian literature and history in preparation for this gathering, and particularly in listening to the papers and discussions of this conference, I have experienced moments of joy and shocks of recognition. But these flashes of illumination—these "Aha Experiences"—should not blind us to several large difficulties facing those attempting comparative studies in western literature and history. Allow me to note a few of these problems.

In the first place, first-rate comparative studies demand thorough acquaintance with two cultures—even at a time when many scholars are convinced they are unable to keep up with the growing amount of scholarship in their areas of specialization. If participants in this conference listened closely to the discussions by American scholars, they will have noticed that we Americans may not be ready to produce full-scale comparative works. The presentations by scholars from south of the border have not delved into Canadian literature and history because we know little about these subjects; until we begin filling these large gaps in our knowledge, our comparisons are likely to be based on inadequate information about Canadian cultures. At this moment, I do not know of a leading scholar of western American literature who is also well versed in Canadian western writing. On the other hand, judging from the papers presented by Canadians at Banff and from several recent essays written by Canadians about their western literature, scholars north of the border are several giant strides ahead of Americans in preparing the way for useful and penetrating studies of the two western literatures.[1]

Another problem concerns definitions. I hope that as we begin to turn out the first extended studies of Canadian and American western writing that we shall fight the tendency to define away geographical and generic exceptions to our new definitions. For example, in trying to define the geographical limits of the American West, several scholars from the United States have excluded California or the Great Plains. In Canada, Edward A. McCourt leaves out British Columbia in his pioneering study, *The Canadian West in Fiction* (1949, 1970). And, on other occasions, interpreters have been inclined to bar such authors as Zane Grey and Ralph Connor from lists of western writers and to categorize them, instead, as producers of subliterary works not worthy of close scrutiny. These attempts to narrow one's focus or to exclude exceptions can be dangerously reductionist. This exclusionist tendency reminds me of two boyhood experiences I had growing up on a sheep ranch in the Pacific Northwest.

My father, a Basque immigrant from Spain, usually purchased white-face Hampshire or black-face Suffolk sheep for his bands; both of these breeds yielded a generous clip of white wool each spring at shearing time. But all of our bands included a few sheep whose wool was dark brown or black. And thus when the shearing crews arrived in the late spring they expected to find a few non-white fleeces—and so did the wool buyer. These dark clips were part of the wool crop; they were an anticipated ingredient.

And another aspect of each band is noteworthy. We always kept a few goats with every flock. I soon learned the reason for the goats. When coyotes or wild dogs attacked a band, sheep tended to turn and run away, and in their flight they exposed their hind legs and tendons to the invaders. But a goat usually turned toward the coyotes and dogs and often chased off the intruders. Thus, when we talked about a band of sheep, we meant a flock that included goats—for, although their actions and personalities varied from those of the sheep, the goats were an essential part of every band. When we spoke of a band of sheep, then, we made room for the black sheep and the goats in our definition.

Too often attempts to limit the focus of western literature have also been efforts to cull out the black sheep and the goats. While it is true, for example, that John Cawelti has provided a new and provocative method for examining the formula Western,[2] future studies should continue comparing and contrasting the Western with other forms of western fiction rather than treating the popular genre as a separate—and usually—inferior type. And though such recent California writers as Richard Brautigan and Joan Didion seem to be dealing with a new kind of West, they too are westerners whose writings are comparable with those of Ken Kesey, Larry McMurtry, and Tom Robbins. Reductionism all too frequently encourages castigation of what it dismisses, and too much is lost in the movement toward exclusion. At this point, at the inception of our comparative work, I hope we can keep the flanks of our roundup as wide as possible. And I am convinced that many of the mavericks we gather will cause us to rethink our restrictive definitions.

Another boundary that the Banff conference has examined is that between literature and history. In the United States, some of the prevailing emphases in research techniques suggest that this boundary is becoming a barrier (although see Professor Don D. Walker's essay in this collection for a contradictory view on this subject). Literary history like that practiced in the much-used *Literary History of the United States* (1948) seems dated to many literary critics; and historians, more than ever, are interested in applying the methods of the social sciences to their disciplines.[3] These recent trends in scholarship bear directly on an important project now under way in western literary history in the United States, and the difficulties involved with this project illuminate problems that similar projects may encounter that attempt to compare literary histories across the border from one another.

The Western Literature Association, organized in the United States in 1965, has recently announced its intention of sponsoring a full-scale literary history of the American West. Selecting an editorial committee of four well-known scholars in western literature, the Association is laying plans for a comprehensive western literary history based on up-to-date findings and thorough research. But one wonders if the committee and the Association are aware of the large difficulties facing them.

Not only are the prevailing winds of scholarship in western American literature and history blowing away from the field of literary history; individual scholars in both fields are not much interested in literary history. When Robert Spiller was chosen to edit the prestigious *Literary History of the United States*, he stressed the importance of the three major ingredients of the project: literary criticism, cultural history, and biography. To judge from books and essays written in the last decade or so about western American literature, scholars in literature åre uninterested in cultural history and biography. Articles in such journals as *Western American Literature, Journal of Popular Culture, South Dakota Review*, and *Southwestern American Literature* reveal the authors' awareness of the American Studies approach of Henry Nash Smith's *Virgin Land: The American West as Symbol and Myth* (1950, 1970), the studies of formula literature by John Cawelti, and the provocative theses of Leslie Fiedler concerning the New Western; but how frequently cited are the older but still very useful works of T. K. Whipple, Lucy Lockwood Hazard, and Franklin Walker? Not very often.[4] And though many specialists in western literature think that western historians are still following closely the ideas and methods of Frederick Jackson Turner, close reading of recent western historiography indicates that such scholars as Ray A. Billington, Earl Pomeroy, Howard Lamar, and John Caughey have either modified or challenged Turner's ideas.

To complicate the issue, western American historians have shown little interest in western literature. Of the dozen or so major western history texts only one or two devote chapters to western writers or use literature as a major source for their generalizations. Occasionally historians devote a session to literary themes in their annual meetings, but no more than a handful of historians are active in the Western Literature Association.

If the kind of comparative study that the Banff conference calls for is to become a reality, the earlier close friendship between Clio and Calliope will have to be rediscovered; the followers of the two muses are currently in danger of not recognizing one another. Where do we go from here? If the spirited and provocative beginnings at Banff are to be continued we need to plan follow-up activities.

The published proceedings of the first gathering will become a necessary base for subsequent discussions, but other meetings should be arranged. Perhaps the following suggestions will be useful for those who try to plan such roundups.

First, a second conference should be organized in the United States some time in the next two or three years. The proceedings of the Banff conference should be an intimate part of this second gathering; possibly one or two sessions could be devoted to the findings of the 1978 conference. The experiences at Banff also indicate that other kinds of advanced planning could be carried out in preparation for another meeting. For example, scholars and participants on both sides of the boundary should be sent bibliographies of the major published commentary on western Canadian and American literature and history. These advanced listings would be particularly useful for those students beginning their comparative work.

In addition, a second meeting should include at least one session devoted to works of literature and history that have attempted to be comparative. Willa Cather, for example, deals with comparative experiences (although not in the Wests) in her *Shadows on the Rock* (1931). More recently, Wallace Stegner in *Big Rock Candy Mountain* (1943) and *Wolf Willow* (1962) writes about his experiences in both countries. And the historian Paul Sharp attempted comparisons in his book *Whoop-Up Country: The Canadian-American West, 1865-1885* (1955), a study which built on the earlier findings in his *Agrarian Revolt in Western Canada: A Survey Showing American Parallels* (1948).

Though most recent writing about American and Canadian literary cultures has emphasized differences between the two countries, we should think more about the possibilities of similarities. As John W. Chalmers of the University of Alberta has written in a review of two recent publications on the Canadian West, "the North American Great Plains, whether north or south of the forty-ninth parallel, is one region, not two, and occasionally might well be examined as such."[5]

And what do studies in geography, political science, sociology, and anthropology have to contribute to scholars in literature and history? The Banff conference did not raise this question, nor did it invite to the meeting political and cultural administrators of the two Wests so that participants might hear what these persons think about the differences and similarities of the two regions. A second meeting would add useful information if it recruited representatives with these backgrounds along with the usual delegations from departments of literature and history.

A summer seminar for teachers would also help encourage Canadian-American western studies. Even more useful would be two seminars—one held in the United States and one in Canada—that brought together college and university teachers wishing to offer courses in western literature. Probably the best method of organization would be to invite fifteen to twenty instructors to an eight-week, team-taught summer seminar that stressed comparisons between western Canadian and American literature and history. These short courses would allow teachers to study and discuss materials suitable for classes to be developed in their home institutions, but the seminars should also give participants an opportunity to write an extended comparative essay. If the second general conference would encourage mature scholars to develop far-reaching comparisons, the summer seminars could aim at preparing a small group of teachers to direct students in courses in comparative literary cultures. Together, the two experiences should expand and extend the enthusiasm kindled here at Banff.

And now let me end where I began—in search of useful symbols. As the turbulence of the sixties has gradually settled in the United States, we realize that some of our cultural archetypes are changing. If Huck Finn thinks he has "got to light out for the territory ahead" at the end of Mark Twain's memorable novel of 1894, the directions and reasons for flight have changed sharply in the last two decades. When Chief Bromden escapes a newly resurrected man from the stultifying combine of a mental institution at the end of Ken Kesey's *One Flew Over the Cuckoo's Nest* (1962), he thinks of heading into Canada—after he has re-examined the western country of his boyhood. Unlike Huck, the Chief will not go west—he will go north. For many western Americans the direction is not now west—or east—but north or south. If nothing else, the Banff conference reveals how much some westerners—perhaps on both sides of the boundary—want to rediscover the meaning of what Grandfather in John Steinbeck's "Leader of the People" calls the westering spirit. Maybe in our quest for this westering spirit we shall learn the important lesson of community that William Stafford suggests in his poem "At the Un-National Monument Along the Canadian Border." At any rate, now that we have seen the elephant, now that we have straightened out our directions and have catalogued our joys and measured our shocks of recognition, it is time to light out for the border ahead—to re-examine the boundaries that separate and join us.

Notes

1   Among the useful recent articles on western Canadian literature are Dick Harrison, ·'Across the Medicine Line: Problems in Comparing Canadian and American Western Fiction," *The Westering Experience in American Literature: Bicentennial Essays*, ed. Merrill Lewis and L. L. Lee (Bellingham, Washington: Western Washington University, 1977), pp. 48-56; Henry Kreisel, "The Prairie: A State of Mind," *Transactions of the Royal Society of Canada*, VI (June 1968), 171-180; Eli Mandel, "Romance and Realism in Western Canadian Fiction," *Prairie Perspectives 2*, ed. A. W. Rasporich and H. C. Klassen (Toronto: Holt, Rinehart and Winston, 1973); W. L. Morton, "Seeing an Unliterary Landscape," *Mosaic*, III (Spring 1970), 1-10; and Rudy Wiebe, "Western Canada Fiction: Past and Future," *Western American Literature*, VI (Spring (1971), 21-30. But the beginning place for the study of western Canadian fiction is now Dick Harrison, *Unnamed Country: The Struggle for a Canadian Prairie Fiction* (Edmonton: University of Alberta Press, 1977).

2   Cawelti's ideas are expressed in his *The Six-Gun Mystique* (Bowling Green, Ohio: Popular Press, 1971), and his full-scale study of popular literary formulas, *Adventure, Mystery and Romance* (Chicago: University of Chicago Press, 1976).

3   I have dealt at more length with problems involved in studying western American history and literature in "Western Fiction and History: A Reconsideration," *The American Frontier*, ed. Jerome Steffen (Norman: University of Oklahoma, 1978), in press.

4   For a recent survey of the commentary on western American literature, see Richard W. Etulain, "The American Literary West and Its Interpreters: The Rise of a New Historiography," *Pacific Historical Review*, XLV (August 1976), 311-348.

5   *Western Historical Quarterly*, XI (April 1978), 239.

Summing Up

Henry Kreisel

I believe I am right in saying that the original conception that led to what turned out to be a magnificent conference was relatively straight-forward and simple. Dick Harrison conceived the idea of bringing together writers, critics, and historians of the two Wests—the American and the Canadian—in order that we might together explore how much we had in common, but also how we differed. The final goal of the conference was the establishing of contacts, the opening up of new intellectual territory and the crossing of the frontiers—geographical, historical, psychological—that separate our two countries.

Many of us have known for a long time that, although we are close neighbors, there are man things about each other that we don't know, and that there are many things that we think we know, only to find out on closer scrutiny that our knowledge is fragmentary and that we rely, to a greater extent than we perhaps dare to acknowledge, on stereotypes and clichés.

The conference achieved a good deal more than I would have dared to expect. It certainly revealed, for me at least, large areas of my own ignorance or misconception, and opened up new frontiers. I believe I am right in saying that my own experience was shared by many of the participants. I did not, for instance, know the work of Frank Waters or Frederick Manfred at all, though they are major novelists of the American West. I would suspect that many of the Canadian participants found themselves in a similar position, and I am certain that most of the American participants did not know the work of such Western Canadian writers as Sinclair Ross, Margaret Laurence, W. O. Mitchell and Rudy Wiebe, to name only a few. I doubt also whether many people at the conference—Americans and Canadians alike—knew the three volumes of poetry (Dorn's *Slinger*, Ondaatje's

Billy the Kid, and Kroetsch's *Seed Catalogue*) that served as center-
piece of Eli Mandel's fine paper "The Border League: American 'West'
and Canadian 'Region.'

In addition, as became painfully clear to me in one of the
panel discussions I attended, there is the enormously interesting field
of "minority literature"—Chicano, native American, Asian-American
in the United States, and the literature produced by so-called "ethnic"
writers in Canada—that is virtually *terra incognita*. Many frontiers
inside the two countries remain to be crossed.

I must say at once that virtually without exception the speakers
at the conference either knew or sensed that the materials they were
analyzing might be unfamiliar to large sections of the audience and
they made sure, therefore, to provide information and context. As a
result, the papers as a whole were the most listenable I have ever heard
at a conference. Speakers really were talking to other *people*, not
simply to an assembled group of specialists.

From the beginning it became clear that the frontiers we might
be crossing would not be primarily geographical, but would be frontiers
that divide disciplines (in this case history and literature) or frontiers
of the mind, frontiers created by differing conceptions and perceptions
of reality. I used the phrase "might be crossing" because I am not at
all sure, on looking back, whether some of these frontiers were in fact
crossed at all. Certainly we approached frontiers of the mind, but did
we cross them? Can they, in fact, be crossed? Even more puzzling:
are there some frontiers that should not be crossed, or cannot be
crossed, however hard we try? Certainly we should be aware of them,
should even approach them, but we might in the end decide not to
cross them.

In a way, though only by implication, the problem was raised
in Don Walker's opening paper, "On the *supposed* frontier between
history and fiction" (italics added). Clearly, Professor Walker indicated
by his title that the frontiers between the disciplines could be crossed.
He saw the frontier between novelists and historians as friendly. There
was, he admitted, a line between them, but this need not be a barbed
wire. What binds fiction and history is human interest. That is the point
where the frontiers meet.

Professor Walker chose the figure of the cowboy as he
appears in history and fiction in order to illustrate the problem and
offer possible solutions. The historian ought to be concerned with the
cowboy's consciousness, but how is he to render that consciousness
in the absence of reliable records? The trail drivers of Texas, said

Walker, provide the richest source materials, but on the whole drivers had neither the time nor the inclination to keep records on the trail, and later recollections inevitably mix nostalgia and fact, dream and reality. How is the historian to deal with this material? Here Professor Walker seemed less certain. He acknowledged that fiction can venture into profound regions of perception where historiography can perhaps not dare to venture, though I got the impression that he would favor the historian crossing the supposed frontier that separates fiction from history. But how far?

In the discussion, difficulties at once manifested themselves. Delbert Wylder, while agreeing that Walker's humanist approach was desirable, reminded us that historians have recently become even more intent on so-called objectivity, and that this implied a move towards "measurement," towards social science. The temperamental frontier between novelist and historian was perhaps wider than Professor Walker would allow.

In one sense, though certainly not by pre-design, Howard Lamar's paper, "The Unsettling of the American West: The Mobility of Defeat," answered some of the questions Walker's paper had raised. Professor Lamar demolished some myths, and drew humanist conclusions from a study of the overland diaries left by the migrants who moved west between 1840 and 1870. A study of the diaries establishes, to begin with, the group character of the wagon trains, as well as the essentially middle-class and Victorian attitudes of people who belonged to similar ethnic, religious, or regional backgrounds.

Lamar's analysis introduced the temperamental frontier that separates men and women who are exposed to the same experience, but react differently to that experience. The overland migration was in general unsettling for women and adventurous for men. For men it was a kind of rite of passage to manhood, and hence the trail experience has a strong masculine emphasis. In American fiction the negative side of Western migration has been largely ignored, for that fiction tended to celebrate the pioneering spirit of the experience and to move the image of America as the new paradise westward. Wandering people, said Lamar, create their own myths. And it is perhaps here, at the point where myth and documented reality meet, I thought, that the historian might most successfully cross the frontier between the disciplines.

Lamar, admittedly after having given himself a crash course in Canadian history and literature, also attempted to delineate the frontiers that separate the Canadian from the American experience. In Canada migration followed the railroad. The character of the groups that settled the Canadian West was also very different. And above all, there is in Canada an absence of the theme of manifest destiny and of the paradisal vision.

Lewis Thomas developed an interesting theory of the nature of the settling of the Canadian West. It was a settlement, Professor Thomas maintained, controlled essentially from the East, so that the Canadian West stood in relation to the East as colony to metropolis. The West was in an entirely dependent position, and the new society was formed in a mould that had to be acceptable to the people who controlled that development from the center and who wanted to see to it that what happened in the West was patterned on the British model. Above all, they did not wish the Canadian West to go the way of the Western United States. They wanted in effect to create strong frontiers and not to cross them.

It was a provocative thesis that did not perhaps take fully into account how the intentions of the center were modified and changed by the settlers, nor did it take fully into account the conflicts that developed between the East and the West and thus set a pattern that continues to this day. Thomas did show, however, as did Lamar also, how the geographical frontier shaped the nature of the economic, social and ultimately psychological development of the two Wests.

By accident or design, but probably by accident, the major literary papers were given by critics who also happen to be creative writers, and we had a dramatic shift of focus which at the same time illuminated the nature of frontiers that were primarily psychological. For whereas the historians had dealt with a West rooted in historical and geographical fact, Robert Kroetsch, Leslie Fiedler, and Eli Mandel gave us a mythical West, a West of the mind, and so, without perhaps intending to, raised the question of whether the historical and the mythic West can be joined, whether the geographical and historically-determined frontiers on the one hand, and the mythic, imaginative frontiers on the other hand could be crossed, and if so, how. No doubt literary historians would have approached the whole question of the frontiers between disciplines in a different manner.

Robert Kroetsch started off with a provocative question: "How do you make love in a new counrty?" His paper, "The Fear of Women in Prairie Fiction," in which he used Willa Cather's *My Antonia* and Sinclair Ross's *As For Me and My House* as jumping-off points, became an extended metaphor for the exploration of male-female relationships in the settlement of a newly-opened continent by men and women who regarded the territory as essentially virgin land, since the indigenous population was pushed aside and became virtually invisible in the scheme of things.

Kroetsch developed a set of interesting, if sometimes fanciful, dichotomies. In his order of things the male stands for external space, the female for internal space. The horse becomes the central symbol for the male, the house for the female, the one denoting movement, the other stability. Men (cowboys, outlaws, often orphans) often feel threatened by the house and all it stands for, and hence travel becomes central in works which are at the same time place-obsessed. One cannot tell the geography of love apart from the geography of fear.

To some extent at least, Howard Lamar's sober analysis of the overland diaries corroborates some of Kroetsch's imaginative leaps, although it is also true, as Sandra Djwa pointed out, that Kroetsch imposed a 1960s view of sexuality on novels written in 1918 and 1940 respectively. I wondered how far historians like Don Walker would be prepared to go in meeting artist-critics like Kroetsch. Put another way: if the historian attempts to penetrate into the cowboy's consciousness, does this inevitably lead him into the region of psycho-history, and what frontiers need to be crossed in a terrain that is full of quagmires?

Kroetsch's West, though fundamentally mythic and psycho-logical, was at the same time still geographically-determined. It had become a theatre in which men and women played out their parts in a game of courting and mating, of attraction and repulsion. In the papers of Leslie Fiedler and Eli Mandel geography and history had receded entirely. They gave us a totally mythic West, a West as a region of the mind.

For Fiedler, who gave his paper the provocative title of "Canada and the invention of the Western," the central myth of the West is embodied in the quintessential American art form—"the Western." This myth bridges all boundaries, since it is in effect the myth of the making of Americans, that is, an account in mythic form of the transformation of Europeans into something other—no longer Europeans, if not yet Americans. Fiedler saw this original dream of the West dreamed by a group of English-speaking explorers before the continent was differentiated. It was a dream of love triumphing over fear, a myth of good companions (first expressed by Alexander Henry), but also a myth of the escape from civilization, a flight from home and from law and order. In the creation of that myth Robert Service becomes for Fiedler the central figure. It is thus a myth invented by a Canadian that has profoundly moved the imagination of Americans,

though not, Fiedler admitted, that of Canadians, at least not to the
same extent.

The elevation of Service into an archetypal figure was, I admit,
somewhat surprising to me, and I am not sure whether it really stands
up to close scrutiny, or whether it was Fiedler's brilliant rhetoric
that made it work, at least as long as one was under his spell.

Eli Mandel moved us even further away from geographical
realities. Canada, to be sure, is a borderline country in which maps
provide some boundaries, but space is the central fact. The borders tend
to blur. An Easterner (Michael Ondaatje) creates a Western myth, a
Canadian (Robert Kroetsch) becomes truly aware of Canada and of
himself as a Canadian by way of the United States. The journey into
the West, into the interior, becomes a space journey, indeed a cosmic
journey. It is a journey that is full of dangers. Some are strong enough
to undertake it (they ride the whirlwind, to use Mandel's phrase),
but others must anchor themselves into a tent if they are to survive.

From geographical frontiers to mythic frontiers; from historical
frontiers to psychic frontiers. That was the road travelled by this conference. The question of whether these frontiers were really friendly
could not ultimately be answered, but that the two Wests still provide
exciting regions of exploration emerged clearly and incontrovertibly.

It was perhaps that sense of excitement, that sense of realization
of the richness of the human experience that is woven into the fabric
of the great Western regions of this continent that turned the conference
at times into a kind of celebration, never more so than when Ken
Mitchell and the Dumptrucks played and sang Western music or when
poets and novelists (Frank Waters and Rudy Wiebe, Dorothy Livesay
and Jack Hodgins, William Stafford and Wallace Stegner, W. O. Mitchell
and Frederick Manfred, Andy Suknaski and Keith Wilson) read to us
of what it is like to live here and to experience this land.

Summing Up

Rosemary Sullivan

A border, as Marshall McLuhan has said, is not a connection but an interval of resonance. In this sense the Crossing Frontiers Conference was a border where two cultures crossed for a brief interval, and there was very much the feeling that this was a beginning, a perusal of the territory before any mapping could be done. Integrating the conference was the concept of the frontier, which came to have several meanings: there was the historical frontier in America in the nineteenth century, and the frontier as a mythic concept which helped give definition to American culture. If the frontier is a useful concept at all for Canada, it describes a different historical experience. The frontier as myth was never a powerful element in cultural definition. By the end of the conference, the word became a pun as all were concerned to identify the new frontiers between the two cultures.

In this experiment in comparative cultural analysis, it was interesting to see that the American scholars were concerned with similarities and the Canadian scholars with differences. The Americans were speaking from a known territory and seemed to be seeking corroboration of endemic patterns. The Canadians were most insistent on differences and were often more familiar than their American colleagues with the counter-reality against which they were defining indigenous identity. The overriding questions were "what is the West(s)?" and "are the West and the frontier synonymous concepts?"

The first border to be crossed was that of language since words have borders. Americans stand on one side of the word "West," Canadians on the other. The American understanding of the word necessarily includes the Turner thesis of the frontier that makes American and West virtually synonymous. The Canadian begins with a confusion between an assumed identity with an American experience and a different historical reality, and is forced to sort out the two. In short, the difference is a romantic versus an ironic identification with the frontier concept, which may be the most important insight into cultural differences reached at Crossing Frontiers.

The frontier, in generic terms, can be seen as a process involving a tension between culture and nature, the accommodation of European cultural norms to a New World wilderness. The American concept of the frontier was given historical definition by Frederick Jackson Turner in his famous address to the American Historical Association in Chicago in 1893. As is well known, the Turner thesis is that the forces of mobility, environment and "free land" helped give form to American attitudes toward individualism and dissent, and therefore ultimately to American democracy. The thesis implies a dynamic of cultural definition. According to it, adaptation of European cultural norms to American environmental realities was gradual. As Americans moved across the continent, divesting themselves of their cultural baggage, they moved through a great variety of environments, and the necessary process of adjustment produced a truly unique civilization. The quintessential American is to be found in the West at the end of this process.[1] The Turner thesis has been attacked for its failure to confront the impact of urbanization, industrialization and class antagonisms, and for its naivete in refusing to see that democracy rests on affluence. Whatever the merits of these criticisms, the thesis remains a powerful one because it defined and perpetuated a myth of the West that captured the popular imagination. It is the familiar myth of idealistic America, a romantic myth of opportunity and youthful rejuvenation, of the Open Road down which the American Adam walks out of civilization into the wilderness. The myth of the frontier is binary: It "encapsulates the opposition of the good against the bad, the west against the east, the simple against the sophisticated, America against all others."[2]

Any historical study of the American West necessarily begins as a sifting of historical fact and myth that demands a dexterous legerdemain. The historians at the conference began by looking at the frontier experience as an historical fact and rejected the popular misconceptions of it as mythic or false. But myths tell truths of a kind, and these historians were concerned to affirm the cultural "truth-value" of the myth of the West. Robin W. Winks defines the historians' dilemma in his monograph, *The Myth of the American Frontier*:

> A myth, Edmund Leach tells us, must be an expression of
> "unobservable realities in terms of observable phenomena"—
> which is to say that myth, by its very nature, is non-rational.
> Historians increasingly are concerned with the non-rational,
> and it is a truism of history that what people believe to be true
> is more important than what 'in fact' actually happened, since
> they act upon their beliefs, not on 'the facts'. This is not
> to say that historians should not also try to discover what
> actually happened, but if their concern is with the way people
> feel about themselves, if they wish to study human motivation,
> if they are entertained by the idea of national character, then
> clearly they must be concerned with what people believe to
> be true as much as with what is true.3

Professor Howard Lamar began at this point of the discrepancy between
what happened and what was believed. He deconstructed the myth of
the West as a "mobility of defeat." Noting that Turner's thesis rested
on an opposition between individual and environment, his paper
insisted on the need to recover cultural context, and his researches
have led him to dispel as myth the absolute tension between nature and
culture in the frontier West. The root character of the migrant was
essentially that of a middle class Victorian whose conventional preoccupations with peer relations, occupation, ethnicity, religion and
family undermine the thesis of lawlessness. Professor Lamar's point is
a simple one: in the process by which myths are measured against
historically verifiable facts, we begin to sort out the ways in which we
have created ourselves. The process of pioneering in America was
elevated into a mystique of national character and, not surprisingly,
it was a myth created by and about men of an age group between late
teens and mid-twenties. The myth caught the idealism of a wandering
people trying to "organize the most deprived past into some meaningful
thing." But it was also an aggressive myth of appropriation, serving a
rhetoric of progress: the shadow side or underbelly of the myth of
opportunity is the reality of exploitation. The development of the
frontier paradoxically records the defeat of rural culture in America,
as Professor Lamar illustrated. Furthermore, the West was itself a
colony, a regional empire of the East within which was to be found
the internal empire of white settlers who made colonial dependants
of the Indians. The quintessential American is in fact an urban product
of a commercial and technological culture, and the frontier myth is the
focus of nostalgia. The final irony is that the frontier was closed as
Turner well knew, even as he formulated his hypothesis.

This exploration of the interface between history and myth was valuable because, even while the facts gave lie to the myths, the psychological importance of myth was acknowledged. We create and are created by our social myths; it is impossible to act outside the universe of myth. In any future cross-cultural dialogue, it will be necessary to compare cultural myths more rigorously and to examine the mythopoeic function itself. It will be necessary to look at the moral ambiguity of myths, that is, their tendency to have positive and negative sides, and at the process by which social myths harden into closed mythologies, into structures of belief. In so doing we may begin to understand the misperceptions that occur between the two cultures.

The questions which preoccupied the Canadian scholars were: what then is the Canadian historical experience of the frontier? and is there a different Canadian psychological West? Though we seem to have imported a model of the frontier from American history, it has little historical basis in Canadian experience. Contemporary Canadian historiography, which was under-represented at the conference, has concluded that there were several frontiers: the French frontier in the New World (1534-1760), the English frontier settlement of Upper Canada (1783-1837), the Western frontier, and the Northern frontier, and that "while there were a series of Canadian frontiers [and physically and chronologically these frontiers paralleled developments in the USA] the total meaning of the frontier experience for Canada was quite different to that for the United States."[4] The Turner thesis is inappropriate to Canada for many reasons. Not only did Canada remain a monarchy, but the forces of "free land" and "free security," and the environmental diversity that are the basis of the thesis were not operative in Canada. The frontier experience in America grew out of the psychology that made independence by revolution possible. When the frontier ceased to be a regional reality, it became a political myth. In Canada, the fact that independence was achieved by evolution, with the imperial tie left intact, meant that Canadians carried westward with them a very different cultural baggage. One of the most exacting problems in the westward expansion was how to accommodate French and English rights. Another was how to protect a western empire against the potentially subversive Americans.

The conference needed to lay more groundwork concerning the "westering process"[5] in Canada. The contributions of Dick Harrison in *Unnamed Country* would have been helpful. Harrison describes a different West from the American, one struggling to maintain its British character, with "little time for anarchy." The West in the nineteenth

and early twentieth century was a hinterland or set of colonies to
Central Canada, tied loosely to Confederation by a national railway
(and it should be remembered that the railway was first used by
Canadian soldiers sent by Ottawa to suppress a Metis rebellion for
local government). Basing his analysis on cultural images recorded
in historical and literary texts, Harrison describes a Western culture
whose motivating ethos was a vision of imperial order rather than
an ideal of freedom. He concluded that, while the American vision
of order was inductive—"order is generated from the immediate
particulars of experience"—the Canadian concept was deductive—
"order descends logically from higher precepts," and emanates from
a remote center of empire.[6] This difference in episteme clearly led
to a different understanding of the tension between individual and
community, nature and culture, and to a collective sensibility that is
less romantic and individualistic, and more conservative in the radical
sense of that word. Many would concur with the following description
of a Canadian ethos, which seeks to affirm the conservative tradition:

> [There is] in the Canadian tradition a longstanding conviction
> that the pursuit of liberty and happiness are not primary
> or exclusive values, that a reverence for what is is more
> important than the conquest of what is, that human life
> is capable of maintaining an organic continuity with the
> environment and that the past is to be broken or changed
> only with great hesitation or caution, and that many of these
> convictions are reflected in traditional Canadian attitudes,
> laws and institutions.[7]

With the help of comparative historians and sociologists, we are beginning
to form a more accurate perception of the similarities and differences
between Canadian and American cultural experience. What is needed
now are methodologies. It is obvious that as countries we share a
colonial past, and this fact should provide a basis for comparison.
Indeed, Louis Hartz in his *Founding of New Societies: Studies in the
History of the U.S., Latin America, South Africa, Canada, Australia*[8]
provided a useful model to explore the maturation of colonial societies,
which helps to focus on how Canadian and American experiences
differ. The dynamic is as follows: the colonial culture begins in dependency on the mother culture, which results in ambiguous self-definition;
the struggle for detachment is coincident with a period of strident
nationalism; if and when the process is completed, it leads to autonomous culture and secure self-definition. If Hartz's model is followed,

America secured detachment as a culture in the mid-nineteenth century, by which time political independence had provided the basis for a confident sense of American identity; in Canada the process of cultural detachment was painfully protracted. For America, the westering process obviously contributed as a catalytic agent in the process of detachment and helped crystallize attitudes toward change and individual authority. Perhaps the strident and naive idealism that is an element of the Westering myth may be explained as a consequence of a desperate need for definition when cultural identity was insecure. In Canada, the process of detachment from the mother culture was much slower because the imperial ties were maintained and then confounded by the influence of the American hegemony in this century. The West was not a catalyst to self-definition. In fact, Canada is still struggling against the political confusions of an ambiguous identity, in large part because we have been careless or inattentive to our own cultural tradition.

It was also interesting to see how, in a conference on American and Canadian Western Literature, the subject of nationalism was inevitably engaged. Many of the American participants seemed to anticipate a strident nationalism and so began with disclaimers against "nationalist and particularist myths that enforce cultural separation." But it would be a failure to understand what is happening in Canada now if it were not seen that nationalism is a necessary and inevitable component in the process of national articulation in which the country is engaged. Historical analogies are risky at best, but Americans might keep in mind that period of nationalism in their own history, the 1850s. Shared goals and political definition were then ambiguous enough to issue in Civil War. Canadians are now in the process of recreating themselves politically, and nationalism provides the energy for self-perception and commitment.

The major emphasis of the conference was to be on literature, and it was therefore appropriate that the literary critics followed the historians with comparative analyses of the two Western literatures. Kroetsch, Mandel and Fiedler were each concerned to explore the myth of the West, and myth, in this sense, meant a narrative defining collective psychology. As Fiedler put it: "Myths are fantasies or waking dreams that alter for a whole body of people not only the perception of reality, but behavior itself." It would have been valuable at this point to have had an analysis of the distinctions between social and literary mythology to facilitate the dialogue between the historians and literary critics.

Fiedler's reading of the myth of the West was familiar from
Return of the Vanishing American. As he writes there, "the heart of
the Western is not the confrontation with the alien landscape, . . . but
the encounter with the Indian." "The Western story in archetypal form
is . . . a fiction dealing with the confrontation in the wilderness of a
transplanted WASP and a radically alien other, an Indian—leading
either to a metamorphosis of the WASP into something neither White
nor Red, . . . or else to the annihilation of the Indian." The transplanted
European becomes "the hunter, the trapper, the frontiersman, the
pioneer, at last the cowboy, . . . the beatnik, the hippie," in search of
aboriginal America.[9] Thus the West for Fiedler is paradoxically placeless.
It is anywhere in the physical globe where men happen to dream new
men in an altered world, and the Western is finally that "dialogue
between whatever old selves we transport out of whatever East and
that radically different other whom we confront in whatever West we
attain."[10] The West is a myth of paradise regained through the archetypal eros of male bonding. Man leaves behind woman, order, and
culture for the aboriginal companion in a romantic confrontation with
the wilderness. It is of course an egocentric myth. In this archetypal
garden, the Indian is only a vehicle to a white version of the self, and
the story ends with his death or disappearance. Fiedler speaks of the
heart of the myth as idealistic: of love triumphing over fear and hatred
of the alien other. But, as he is well aware, the other is most often
perceived as a projection of something in the white psyche, either fear
or wish, and nature is seen as raw material for the heroic engagement.
The position of woman is also revealing. It is she who keeps man from
the wilderness, which explains the misogyny of the Western myth.
Fiedler roused considerable antagonism in some of his listeners perhaps
because he became the didactic critic speaking out of the heart of the
myth, insisting on interpreting the Other to the Other. While Fiedler
certainly sees the solipsism of the myth, his objectivity seemed com-
promised by the romantic possibilities of the dream, and he can be
faulted for a failure of irony. The problem is complex but worth
pursuing because paradigmatic. Fiedler insisted that Canada and America
shared the same myth of the West (the archetypal eros of male bonding):
Thoreau got it from Alexander Henry. The Canadians who spoke in
response said "no"—the Canadian experience is not essentially that.
Fiedler's response made it clear that he didn't understand or simply
couldn't hear these disclaimers because, after all, this was an idealistic
myth of love triumphing over fear and hatred of the alien other. But
of course the real paradox of the myth is that the other is given no

voice and must accept definition. For all its idealism, the myth is arrogant and solipsistic in its assumption that there can only be one dream and all else is vehicle to the dreamer.

Gary Snyder, in a recent essay, "The Incredible Survival of Coyote," writes that the West is over, and Western American writers are engaged in a fundamental revision of the old myth. I quote at length Snyder's version of what Western literature has been:

> The West as it's talked about seems to me to be concerned with the history of literature of the period of exploitation and expansion west of the tree line, and of course this is what they mean when they talk about the epic or heroic period of the West. It's a period of rapid expansion, first phase exploitation. It is not a literature on history of place, I think. It's a history and a literature of feats of strength and of human events; of specifically white, English-speaking-American human events. It's only about the West by accident, about this place by accident. . . .
>   The West, then, presented us with an image of manliness, of vigor, of courage, of humor, of heroics which became a very strong part of our national self-image; perhaps the strongest part, the most pervasive, the one which has been most exported to the rest of the world. There are, of course, Southern images: the Daniel Boone image, there is the Yankee self-image and several others in American folk literature/folk lore history. But the Western image, which is a kind of amalgam of mountain man, cowboy, and rancher is one of the strongest self-images of America. The West ceases to be (whether it's geographically Western or not) when economy shifts from direct, rapid exploitation to a stabilized agricultural recycling base. Heroics go with first phase exploitation, hence, fur industry, then cattle industry, then mining, then logging.[11]

According to Snyder, a new literature is evolving to meet the need for a new ethos. The literature has changed from a literature of a period of exploitation and expansion to a literature of *place*. This literature of place is different from regional literature, which features stories of particular human habits and ethnic diversities. Its muse is the Trickster, Coyote, who is anti-heroic and morally ambivalent; its subject is the land; and it is more interested in aboriginal than in white culture and in mythic than in historical time. It is clearly a literature of survival appropriate to an ecologically conscious age in quest of harmony with local place and way of life. It is interesting, however, that it retains the curious dualism that to Canadians seems anti-social, the fierce and exclusive opposition between nature and culture, and that the focus of change remains the individual. The essentially new element is the reconception of the relationship to the Other, where the land and the Indian (though not always woman or foreigner) poses the challenge: can the Other be known in and for itself and not as a vehicle to one's own apocalyptic myth?

Nineteenth- and early twentieth-century Western Canadian literature is different from traditional Western American literature because there never has been a frontier literature. The heart of the literature is the encounter with the land, and not the homoerotic bonding of white with Indian or the myth of frontier freedom. Dick Harrison has written that:

> The West to be found in English Canadian fiction is rarely a "frontier." If a "frontier" is taken to be that meeting point of advancing civilization and untamed nature, where civilized order confronts unordered wilderness, then there is no reason to expect one, since the frontier era was virtually over by the time the literature began. The fur traders and the missionaries had been operating in the West under what might be called frontier conditions for two hundred years by the time the first western novel, Begg's *Dot it Down*, was published in 1871. When most of the early novelists began to come west with the bulk of settlement from Ontario, Great Britain, and the American Middle West, they came into incredibly rigorous pioneer conditions, but not to the edge of a trackless wilderness. They had the sense of a plain patrolled by the North West Mounted Police, surveyed for settlement, with a railroad stretching out to cross it. They were not on the edge of anything; they were surrounded by something, and they took it to be the civilized order they had always known. . . .
>
> Central Canada was not looking to an advancing frontier to provide its identity or mature its character. There was little demand for a frontier myth in the Canadian consciousness of the time. Central Canada was not, of course, an Atlantic nation seeking independence, but a landlocked nation struggling to maintain its British character. Because the West was hardly more to her than a source of land, markets, and raw materials, the settlers—and the novelists —could not think of themselves as being at the source of historical forces shaping their nation.
>
> As a result, whatever ideals of nationhood appear in the fiction of the early Twentieth Century are attuned to the preservation of an empire which has already asserted its dominion over the land, and which has its centre somewhere

else. Frontier values of individualism and egalitarianism are
evident, but greatly tempered by faith in a higher, intangible
order.12

The myth that did surface in early Western Canadian literature was
what might be called a myth of imperial order. Rather than the image
of the lone cowboy one finds the mountie, and the image of the frontier
is replaced by the image of a garden:

> This, the archetypal garden, is the most common though not
> often the most convincing image of the prairie in the stories of
> Ralph Connor, Nellie McClung, Arthur Stringer, the early
> R. J. C. Stead, and a host of less popular romancers of their
> time. Like Eden their West had no [indigenous] past, only a
> present beginning when the settler arrives, and a better future.
> This was, of course, a time of boom and optimism and, for the
> writers at least, a time of agrarian ideals. The free independent
> farmer is in their eyes the most productive citizen and likely
> to be the happiest and most virtuous because of the ennobling
> effects of his honest labour and continual contact with nature.
> Nature is a divine order in almost the eighteenth century sense,
> exacting harsh service of man but ultimately beneficient.13

The image of the West as a kind of Eden where the New Adam might
have a second chance seems to be shared by Western American and
Canadian literature, but there is a difference; and this, according to
Harrison, is in the contrasting visions of human order identified in
the relationship between man and nature that are embodied in the
Frontier and Garden myths. In Canadian Western fiction there is a
"hazy identification of the human order of empire, the natural order,
and the divine order," in short, a myth of benevolent imperialism.

If, as Snyder says, American writers are deconstructing the
Western myth of the frontier, Canadian writers are identifying and
deconstructing the imperial myth, which is seen as morally simplistic
and fundamentally irresponsible to local place. It is interesting to see
how the two "new" literatures meet in commitment to place, but,
as Eli Mandel indicated in his paper "The Border League: American
'West' and Canadian 'Region,'" there remains a profound, if subtle,
difference—the difference between a spiritual quest and an ancestral
dream. The archetypal hero of American Western literature remains
the nomadic trickster, less dangerously innocent now that his romantic
ego is trimmed by a conviction of the diminishment of human possibilities, but still essentially in pursuit of that dream of intensity offered by

the territory ahead. When the territory outside failed, he turned inward in search of adventure. The frontier psychology thus survives with all its impossible longing for freedom and for a world, as F. Scott Fitzgerald wrote, commensurate to man's capacity for wonder. It is the dream of America.

The archetypal hero of Western Canadian fiction dreams, according to Kroetsch, a "dream of origins," of ancestral roots. As Mandel makes clear, the important thing is that the Western writer dreams not of real places but of remembered places, seeking to offer an explanation of where we come from. Thus he creates myths which reject a colonial version of the past and a long standing cultural diffidence, in favor of what can only be called a love of his region. He is modern enough to be made nervous by patriotism—what he seeks is to be "at home in a native space." The poetic or fictional forms the writer turns to are often catalogues or documentary narratives because a process of cultural anthropology is involved in the effort to recover cultural memory. Such forms are used to strip away a false overlay of received versions of the self in order to find what is true and what is false; or, as Kroetsch explained it, "demythologizing the systems that threaten to define [you]."[14] The Western novelist Margaret Laurence is typical in writing: "Many Canadian writers, myself among them, have spent much of our lives, in our novels and poems, coming back home, in a spiritual sense, trying to bring into acknowledged being the myths and backgrounds and places which belong to us."[15] And Rudy Wiebe has said: "The principal task of the Canadian writer is not simply to explain his contemporary world, but to create a past, a lived history, a vital mythology."[16]

We had at the conference an example of a writer engaging in this process of deconstruction. Robert Kroetsch's paper "The Fear of Women in Prairie Fiction" was an act of criticism as fictional autobiography, and it had less to do with Ross and Cather than with the myth of the West. As a border man, Kroetsch began by demythologizing the myth that threatens to define him—the American cowboy myth. With a typical Canadian irony, he turned the romantic, energetic myth into a myth of impotence. He rephrased the binary distinctions between nature and culture, man and woman, west and east, as an opposition between horse and house, and like a good Canadian, was unable to see these except as equally matched opposites in mutual dependency. In contrast, the mythic American cowboy believes he can light out for the territory ahead leaving the house in the dust of his horse's hoofs and seems continually surprised when Aunt Sally catches up with him.

The Canadian, as Kroetsch sees, has circled the house. He couldn't light out for the territory ahead and he couldn't enter the house, so he exhausted himself in the compromise of the horse-house. But as a member of the audience quipped, "he who sits on the fence gets a sore Kroetsch." With brilliance and agony, Kroetsch reads the Canadian dilemma. He sees the cowboy vision of the West as male obedience to a solipsistic version of the self that protects distance and diffidence —the male as cowboy, outlaw, orphan, defines himself out of all possibility of entry to the house.[17] What, we ask, is the cowboy protecting? His version of freedom—the possibility of continuous and radical beginning. The house stands in his mind for fixity and limitation, a submission of self to choice. So he feeds and feeds his fear of women, delighting in the near miss. But Kroetsch sees the paradox here as he turns the old myth upside down. In fleeing women, it was supposed that the cowboy fled order and control. In Kroetsch's version, woman is the unknown chaos, and man holds on to the known and safe by resisting her. He is protecting his "precious and . . . treacherous *name.*" The challenge is to be unnamed, to abandon those versions of the heroic self which preclude seeing the other as anything but a limitation to the self. Kroetsch has spoken elsewhere of the "outrageous, seductive, fabulated . . . vision of what total freedom must be," and this is clearly the romantic myth of America. But it is a myth he can't believe in. He circles the house.

The problem that the Canadian writer has now posed to himself is how to be freed from freedom. At this crucial point the new Canadian myth emerges. It is not a myth of pursuit of the territory ahead, it is a communal myth of return, of homecoming. "You can't go home again; you must go home again," as Margaret Laurence puts it. Our epic of the West, Rudy Wiebe's *Scorched Wood People* is a myth of settlement, describing a collective experiment in legitimate self-government. The story is prophetic because it is motivated by a religious vision of a possible paradise that fails in the realization but remains in the mind as an impossible dream of human fulfillment. The book is not an apocalyptic version of imaginative survival in flight from society, nor are we in that part of the American imagination where man seeks a new world commensurate to his capacity for wonder. On the frontier the Canadian always turns back to accept the compromises of the world and his participation in it. To the American dream he opposes an anti-romantic or ironic myth of communal order. The poet Doug Jones sees this ironic perspective as essentially Canadian. "One could cite a variety of writers, critics and historians to suggest the degree to which Canadian life and culture have been characterized by an ironic awareness, a play of paradoxes and ironic tensions—between French and English, the bush and the salon, Europe and America —making royalists nationalists and nationalists either regionalists or internationalists—creating a policy of compromise, an identity of difference."[19] When we look to the two cultures do we then see a romantic or apocalyptic versus an ironic version of the self, complimentary but essentially different perceptions, each with its positive and negative elements?

We learn much from how we choose to tell our stories, and the most entertaining anecdote of the conference crystallized the difference between the romantic and ironic sensibility. Professor Walker reported reading innumerable journals and diaries of American cowboys written while they were on cattle trecks, and he remarked on the reports of the death and burial of trampled cowboys. These were for him narratives of man's heroic confrontation with the environment and his own mortality. He commented that Canadian journals and diaries recorded no such incidents. A Canadian responded that in fact there were such narratives of cattle trecks and humorously recounted one story of a cattle treck to the Yukon where not the men —but the cattle—froze to death in the winter landscape and the frozen carcasses were shipped north. If you allow enough of an interval of resonance, it is possible to see this as the same human story, but seen from different sides of the border.

Notes

1   Robin W. Winks, *The Myth of the American Frontier: Its Relevance to America, Canada, and Australia* (Leicester: Leicester University Press, 1971), pp. 9-10.

2   Winks, p. 8.

3   Winks, p. 7.

4   Winks, p. 20.

5   This was a phrase used often at the conference; unlike *frontier*, it has no borders.

6   Dick Harrison, *Unnamed Country: The Struggle for a Canadian Prairie Fiction* (Edmonton: University of Alberta Press, 1977), p. 79.

7   D. G. Jones, "In Search of Canada: Dennis Lee's Ironic Vision," *ARC I* (Spring 1978), 24.

8   Louis Hartz, *The Founding of New Societies: Studies in the History of the United States, Latin America, South Africa, Canada, and Australia* (New York: Harcourt, Brace and World, 1964).

9   Leslie A. Fiedler, *The Return of the Vanishing American* (New York: Stein and Day, 1968), pp. 21-24.

10   Fiedler, p. 186.

11   Gary Snyder, "The Incredible Survival of Coyote," *Western American Literature*, 9 (1975), 261.

12   Harrison, pp. 73-74.

13   Harrison, p. 33.

14   Robert Kroetsch, "Unhiding the Hidden: Recent Canadian Fiction," *Journal of Canadian Fiction*, 3:3 (1974), 43-45.

15   "You can almost hear the skipping rope slapping" (review of Dennis Lee's *Alligator Pie*), *Toronto Globe and Mail*, October 5, 1974.

16   David L. Jeffrey, "Biblical Hermenentic and Family History in Contemporary Canadian Fiction: Wiebe and Laurence," *Mosaic*, XI:3 (Spring 1978), 88.

17   Kroetsch, "Fear of Women in Prairie Fiction: An Erotics of Space," this work.

18   "Unhiding the Hidden," p. 44.

19   Jones, p. 27.

Summing Up

Max Westbrook

As a member of the panel charged with the task of summing up
"Crossing Frontiers," I find that my job is not to decide what "grade"
to assign. The conference was extraordinarily successful, probably the
most stimulating I have ever attended. The question, it seems to me,
is *why*. What happened at "Crossing Frontiers," and why was the
conference so successful?

Professor R. T. Harrison had a good idea. That's the beginning.
Comparing and contrasting the literature and history of the Canadian
frontier and the frontier of the United States is an important undertaking, and yet very little work had been done. Thus there was a need
to begin. The site was well chosen. Banff is an unusually attractive
area in a beautiful part of Canada, and for scholars and writers studying
Western frontiers an appropriate setting is a physical document or
lesson, something more than just pleasant surroundings. "Crossing
Frontiers" was generously supported, the enabling act which made it
possible for a large number of professors of English and history, for
poets and novelists, from Canada and the United States, to meet and
work together. Professor Harrison and his staff were courteous and
efficient. The Canadian hosts in general were warm and hospitable,
so much so that one American literary critic—famous for his ability
to start and finish a good academic fight—found himself laughingly
apologizing for being so peaceful.

That's all well and good and much appreciated, but it doesn't
answer the question.

Having reflected at some length on my notes and memories,
I conclude that "Crossing Frontiers" was an unusually rewarding
conference because the fine potentials established by the planning
and execution sparked a spirit of unity *and* independence. There was

no catering, no misplaced and sentimental courtesy of the type that stops honest discussion, and yet the differences that arose were analyzed and discussed with a healthy frankness. Canadians spoke *as* Canadians but *to* citizens of the United States, and this combination of unity and independence was reciprocated. Men and women, poets and novelists, and historians and literary critics maintained their own integrity while engaged in studies of the frontiers of two nations.

So pervasive was this spirit that I found myself in animated conversation with a Canadian professor of history who seemed—to my country eye—a Duke or Lord or something, affable and unbiased, but a born aristocrat. I say "country eye" because I grew up in the woods, learned to read by coal oil lamp, and to this day pronounce "soil" as "saul." Yet neither one of us apologized for his birth or felt any need to resist the birth of the other. On that basis, you have a better chance to learn something.

With national and personal identities accepted and not in jeopardy, it is easier to focus on a profound similarity between the two frontier experiences. The American novelist Frank Waters struck the first note when he told the story of a man who struggled to dig precious metal from mountains, who fought nature and luck, and came to see, finally, that the mountain is within himself. In a quite different way, Canadian novelist Jack Hodgins harmonized with Frank Waters by reading from a novel of comic and serious human energy in motion. Both artists were devoted in their work to the specific locale chosen, and yet the universal tone of both was immediately shared by all.

Outside the conference room, as we listened, was Tunnel Mountain, and I found myself wondering what the Mountain would say if we could find a place to stand and a way to ask, "What nationality are you?" The land, in Alberta or New Mexico, especially a frontier land, is often specific, perhaps unique, for the individual; but wind and rain are not Catholic, Protestant, or Jewish. There is no such thing as a meta-structuralist sunset or a new critical moon. The West of the United States and the Canadian West include God's staggering variety; and Westerners, with their own varieties of courage and failure, are people who respect the challenge of mountain and desert.

To note something common about the experiences of different peoples from distinct nations, of course, is but a beginning. "Crossing Frontiers," however, *was* in many ways a beginning, an academic and literary exploration mapping out the territory up ahead. Professor R. T. Harrison's brief remarks on some differences, for example, are a provocative example. The political independence of Canada, Professor Harrison reminded us, came about through governmental evolution; political independence in the United States resulted from revolution. Everyone knows that, of course, but Professor Harrison was asking about the unexplored implications of this signal difference; and the richness of his question was illustrated by certain parts of Professor Lewis Thomas's paper. Professor Thomas contrasted the impersonal or group hero of Canada—the Mounted Police, for example, but no specific or named individual hero—with the love of the personal and single hero in the West of the United States. In a similar vein, charts for future work were indicated by discussions of other frontiers and boundaries: men and women and the loss or discovery of love on the frontier, history and literature and the puzzling relation between the authentic and the imagined.

Something essential to the discussion of these and other topics was contained, I think, in the recurrent references to *As for Me and My House*, by Sinclair Ross, and *The Scarlet Letter*, by Nathaniel Hawthorne. Mrs. Bentley, from the Canadian side, is married to a good but intellectual and puritanical minister. Hester, whose story is set in the Eastern United States but at a period when the East was the frontier, bears a child of Dimmesdale, a good but intellectual and puritanical minister. Thus the two novels provide a convenient point of comparison.

Mrs. Bentley and Hester have both been accused of wanting to lead their husbands astray. Both are said to be, according to some readers, temptations, the female as corrupt by nature, luring the good husband away from restraint and duty. In both novels, the rules of religion are strict, the times are hard, and there is a pressing need to assert civilization against the wilderness, to create decency on an insecure frontier. The passionate—in the woods and within the self —is welcomed by the two women but held at bay by the stern righteousness of the two ministers.

I am skipping the extensive differences between the two novels, but fairly, I think, since the analogy which came up so frequently in the conference is legitimate.

The interesting thing to me—and I intend this as illustrative, partial, not as inclusive—is that the frontier sensibility in Canada and in the United States suggests a reading that varies from the customary.

If we confront reality in mountain and desert—the literal frontier and the frontiers within ourselves—then the restraint of Mr. Bentley and of Mr. Dimmesdale is a devotion to the not-real, to not-living. The narrowness of the Puritan, the splendid but metaphysically feeble intellect, and the destructive separation of body and flesh come to represent a defeat of the human spirit, not a noble triumph of civilization over the savage.

What does it mean for Mrs. Bentley to invite her husband to love? What does it mean for Hester to invite Dimmesdale to flee with her to a farther frontier? The usual answer is, in its most polite formulation, escapism. Going West—by implication, some times directly so—is associated with running away, with flight from the mature challenge of city and civilization. It is Huck Finn, running away one more time.

"Crossing Frontiers" included this general reading of Mrs. Bentley and Hester, but it included, also, a quite different suggestion. Mr. Bentley's most characteristic habit is to go to his study and shut the door, supposedly to read or write or paint. In fact, he is shutting out life. He is—and I don't mean this metaphorically—burying himself. Dimmesdale's most characteristic habit is to contemplate confession of adultery, to painfully reflect on his guilt, to determine himself to confess in public, and then to deliver a sermon in which he does not confess. Quite literally, he is punishing himself—unto death—in a way which, as he knows, cannot lead to expiation. Both ministers, in brief, commit themselves to *not*-living.

In terms of a frontier concept of reality then, the supposedly destructive passion of Mrs. Bentley and Hester is in fact an invitation to life. Both, with Eastern bias set aside, are revealed as warm and responsible human beings. In the dull and Eastern world of James Fenimore Cooper's fiction, going West is escapism. In a few hundred Hollywood movies, going West is escapism or progress or adventure or the triumph of materialism over savagery or, more recently, another sham heroism to be exposed. And there may well be bits of truth in these and other common Western themes. But Mrs. Bentley and Hester may also serve to teach us what they could not teach their death-loving husbands: the variety of the world includes the variety of the frontier, mountain and desert, body and soul, mind and spirit, the wild and the disciplined.

Again, I don't mean to sum up too narrowly. There is no single myth in the West of the United States and—I'm told and fully believe— no single myth in the Canadian West; but one important myth among many is the story of a Westering spirit, a search, a willingness to confront the original world and yet maintain the self as a rational human being.

Howard Lamar and Sandra Djwa—though neither should be packaged under the one topic I've chosen to emphasize—can be seen as contributing to this direction. Jack Hodgins, Frederick Manfred, and Keith Wilson—each in his own way—may serve to indicate contributions made by creative writers.

There is space in God's world, to put it briefly, for all our differences: national, intellectual, sexual, artistic. And there is also—in the still unexplored frontiers of human experience—a recurrent devotion to the original world, a world that is obscured by categories but explained—somewhat—by the mountain, by the Westering experience.

Biographical Notes on Contributors

Contributors of Major Papers

Leslie Fiedler
Samuel L. Clemens Professor of English
State University of New York
Buffalo, New York

Dr. Fiedler is as well known as any commentator on American literary culture. His best-known publications are *Love and Death in the American Novel* (1960) and *The Return of the Vanishing American* (1968). Dr. Fiedler is also an author of fiction, including *The Last Jew in America*, a novel about Jews in the American West.

Robert Kroetsch
Professor of English
State University of New York
Binghamton, New York

Dr. Kroetsch is a major Canadian novelist who was raised in Alberta and has been teaching in the United States for several years. His novels include *But We are Exiles* (1965), *The Words of My Roaring* (1966), *The Studhorse Man* (winner of the Governor General's Award for 1969), *Gone Indian* (1973), *Badlands* (1975), and *What the Crow Said* (1978). Dr. Kroetsch has also published several volumes of poetry, including *The Ledger* (1975), *Stone Hammer Poems* (1975), and *Seed Catalogue* (1977). He is also co-editor of *Boundary 2, A Journal of Post-modern Literature.*

Howard R. Lamar
W. R. Coe Professor of History
Yale University
New Haven, Connecticut

Dr. Lamar is co-editor with Dr. Ray Billington of the major series "Histories of the American Frontier." His own books include *Dakota Territory, 1861-1889* (1956), *The Far Southwest, 1850-1912* (1966), and *The Trader on the American Frontier* (1977). He is currently working on a book about overland trails in the West.

Eli Mandel
Professor of English
York University
Toronto, Ontario

Dr. Mandel is both a scholar and a western Canadian poet of distinction. His volumes of poetry include *Fuseli* (1960), *Black and Secret Man* (1964), *An Idiot Joy* (winner of the Governor General's Award for 1967), *Crusoe* (1973), *Stony Plain* (1973), and *Out of Place* (1977). His volumes of criticism include *Criticism: The Silent Speaking Words* (1966), *Irving Layton* 1969), and *Another Time* (1977), which includes several germinal articles on Western Canadian literature.

Lewis G. Thomas
Professor of History
University of Alberta
Edmonton, Alberta

Dr. Thomas is well known as an historian of the Canadian West. His book *The Liberal Party in Alberta: A History of Politics in the Province of Alberta, 1905-1921* appeared in 1959 and in 1973 he published a new and now thoroughly documented edition of A. S. Morton's *History of the Canadian West to 1870-71*. He is the author of many essays and articles, particularly on the social and church history of the Canadian West.

Don D. Walker
Professor of English
University of Utah
Salt Lake City, Utah

Dr. Walker is widely known as a teacher and scholar of western American literature. He has published extensively in such journals as *Western American Literature, New Mexico Quarterly, Arizona and the West*, and *American Quarterly*. Dr. Walker was a student of Henry Nash Smith, and both editors of *Western American Literature* have been Dr. Walker's students. He has edited *The Possible Sack*, a journal of commentary on western American literature, and is at work on book-length studies of "The Mountain Man" and "The Cowboy." Dr. Walker is himself a writer of Western short stories.

Commentators

Jack Brenner
Professor of English
University of Washington
Seattle, Washington

Dr. Brenner, during a varied and unconventional academic career, has
published several essays on western subjects, including "Wright Morris's
West . . ." and "Imagining the West."

Sandra Djwa
Professor of English
Simon Fraser University
Burnaby, British Columbia

Dr. Djwa has published widely in the field of Canadian literature and
has edited a selected edition of the poetry of Charles Heavysege. Her
E. J. Pratt: The Evolutionary Vision appeared in 1974. "False Gods
and the True Covenant: Thematic Unity Between Margaret Laurence
and Sinclair Ross," is one of her many essays on prairie fiction.

Richard Etulain
Professor and Chairman of the Department of History
Idaho State University
Pocatello, Idaho

Dr. Etulain's scholarship extends from the history to the literature of
the American West, and particularly the literary history. His publications
include *Owen Wister* (1973), *Western American Literature: A Bibliography of Interpretive Books and Articles* (1972), and *The Popular
Western*, ed. (1974).

Henry Kreisel
University Professor of Comparative Literature
University of Alberta
Edmonton, Alberta

Dr. Kreisel is a prominent western Canadian novelist, whose work includes *The Rich Man* (1948), *The Betrayal* (1964), and short stories appearing in various magazines and anthologies. His "The Prairie: A State of Mind" (1968) is a germinal article on Canadian prairie fiction which is still widely read and respected.

William H. New
Professor of English
University of British Columbia
Vancouver, British Columbia

Dr. New is the editor of *Canadian Literature*, a recognized authority on Malcolm Lowry, and has published a large variety of critical essays, many of which were collected as *Articulating West: Essays on Purpose and Form in Modern Canadian Literature* (1972).

Earl Pomeroy
Professor and Chairman of the Department of History
University of California—San Diego
La Jolla, California

Dr. Pomeroy is a leading historian of the American West. For several years before occupying his present post, he held the Beekman Chair of History at the University of Oregon. In addition to several provocative articles, he has produced books on western territorial history, the islands of the Pacific, and tourism in the West. His most widely-known book is *The Pacific Slope* (1965, 1973).

Rosemary Sullivan
Professor of English
Erindale College, York University
Toronto, Ontario

Dr. Sullivan has published essays on subjects from both sides of the border, on Margaret Atwood, James Dickey, and P. K. Page. Her *Theodore Roethke: The Garden Master* appeared in 1976.

Max Westbrook
Professor of English
University of Texas
Austin, Texas

Dr. Westbrook is a noted student of literary theories and their applications to western American literature. In addition to numerous articles on a variety of literary topics, he has written *Walter Van Tilburg Clark* (1970).

Delbert Wylder
Professor of English
Murray State University
Murray, Kentucky

Dr. Wylder is one of the co-founders of the Western Literature Association and has written several essays on western literary topics. In addition to a highly-praised book on Hemingway's heroes, Professor Wylder has recently completed a study of the western novelist Emerson Hough.

Program of Conference

Organizing Committee
Dick Harrison, chairman
Morton Ross, deputy chairman
Richard Etulain, US liaison

Douglas Barbour
Gerald McCaughey
Beverly Mitchell
Fred Radford
Stephen Scobie
Robert Solomon
Sara Stambaugh
John Thompson
Janis Watkin
Rudy Wiebe
Dale Wilkie

Conference Design
Bruce Bentz
Christopher Ozubko
Department of Art and Design
University of Alberta

Support Staff
John De Wacht
Richard Driskill
Carol Roberts
Janis Watkin
All of the University of Alberta

Wednesday   April 12

Registration

Publishing in the West
*A round table discussion
among western Canadian and
American publishers*
David Gilbert
University of Nebraska Press
L. E. S. Gutteridge
University of Alberta Press
George Melnyk
NeWest Press
Rob Sanders
Western Producer Prairie Books

Readings
by western novelists
Frank Waters
Rudy Wiebe

Reception

Thursday   April 13

Introduction

Major Paper
*On the Supposed Frontier
Between History and Fiction*
Don D. Walker
University of Utah
Chairman: James K. Folsom
University of Colorado

Discussion
with response by
Delbert Wylder
Murray State University

Luncheon
for all delegates

Major Paper
The Unsettling of the American West: The Mobility of Defeat
Howard R. Lamar
Yale University
Chairman: Richard Etulain

Discussion
with response by
Earl Pomeroy
University of California,
San Diego

Coffee

Major Paper
Prairie Settlement: Western Responses in History and Fiction; Social Structures in a Canadian Hinterland
Lewis G. Thomas
University of Alberta
Chairman: David Hall
University of Alberta

Discussion

Readings
by Western Novelists and Poets
Dorothy Livesay
Jack Hodgins
William Stafford
Wallace Stegner

Friday   April 14

Major Paper
The Fear of Women in Prairie Fiction: An Erotics of Space
Robert Kroetsch
SUNY, Binghamton
Chairman: George Baldwin
University of Alberta

Discussion
with response by
Sandra Djwa
Simon Fraser University

Coffee

Panel Discussions
1. Comparing Frontiers in History
John Foster
University of Alberta
Allan Smith
University of British Columbia
Turrentine Jackson
University of California, Davis

2. Freedom and Order on the Frontier
James K. Folsom
University of Colorado
Michael Peterman
Trent University
Rod McLeod
University of Alberta

3. Woman in Western Literature
Lorraine McMullen
University of Ottawa
Susan Wood
University of British Columbia
Barbara Meldrum
University of Idaho

4. Western Poetry
Gary Geddes
University of Alberta
Stephen Scobie
University of Alberta
Thomas Lyon
Utah State University

5. Relationships With Minority Literatures
Elaine Newton
York University
E. D. Blodgett
University of Alberta
Priscilla Oaks
California State University,
Fullerton

Lunch

Major Paper
Canada and the Invention of the Western: A Meditation on the Other Side of the Border
Leslie Fiedler
SUNY, Buffalo
Chairman: Merrill Lewis
Western Washington
State University

Discussion
with response by
Jack Brenner
University of Washington

Coffee

Panel Discussions

6. Historical and Mythic Wests
Brian Dippie
University of Victoria
Douglas Owram
Universiity of Alberta
Kent Steckmesser
California State University,
Los Angeles

7. Man in his Natural Environment
David Carpenter
University of Sasakatchewan
Jane Nelson
Texas A&M University
Bernice Slote
University of Nebraska

8. Native People in Western Literature
Robert Gish
University of Northern Iowa
David Arnason
University of Manitoba
Charles Adams
University of Nevada, Las Vegas

9. Popular Literature of the West
Glen Love
University of Oregon
Laurence Ricou
University of Lethbridge
Michael Marsden
Bowling Green University

10. Literature and Film in the West
Tony Arthur
California State University,
Northridge
Thomas Radford
National Film Board
James Belson
Sun Valley Center
for the Arts and Humanities

Readings
by Western Novelists and Poets
two concurrent sessions
W. O. Mitchell
Frederick Manfred
Andy Suknaski
Keith Wilson

Cocktails

Banquet
with entertainment
Crossing Frontiers
Ken Mitchell and
The Dumptrucks

Saturday   April 15

Major Paper
*The Border League: American
"West" and Canadian "Region"*
Eli Mandel
York Univeristy
Chairman: Peter Buitenhuis
Peter Buitenhuis
Simon Fraser University

Discussion
with response by
W. H. New
University of British Columbia

Coffee

Plenary Panel
Summing Up
Richard Etulain
Idaho State University
Henry Kreisel
University of Alberta
Rosemary Sullivan
Erindale College
Max Westbrook
University of Texas

Luncheon
for major speakers

Tours of Banff and vicinity

List of Conference Speakers with Addresses

Jack Brenner
English Department
University of Washington
Seattle, Washington 98195

Sandra Djwa
Department of English
Simon Fraser University
8888 Barnet Highway
North Burnaby, British Columbia
V5A 1S6

Richard Etulain
Department of History
Idaho State University
Pocatello, Idaho 88605

Leslie A. Fiedler
Department of English
SUNY Buffalo
Buffalo, New York 14260

Jack Hodgins
Rutherford Road
RR 1
Lantzville, British Columbia
V0R 2H0

Henry Kreisel
Department of Comparative Literature
University of Alberta
Edmonton, Alberta T6G 2E1

Robert Kroetsch
Department of English
SUNY Binghamton
Binghamton, New York 13901

Howard R. Lamar
Department of History
Yale University
New Haven, Connecticut 06520

Dorothy Livesay
CVII, Box 32
University Centre
University of Manitoba
Winnipeg, Manitoba
R3T 1E0

Eli Mandel
Department of English
York University
4700 Keele Street
Downsview, Ontario
M3J 1P3

Frederick Manfred
RR 3
Luverne, Minnesota 56156

Ken Mitchell
Department of English
University of Regina
Regina, Saskatchewan
S4S 0A2

W. O. Mitchell
73 McRae Drive
Toronto, Ontario
M4G 1S3

William New
Department of English
University of British Columbia
Vancouver, British Columbia
V6T 1W5

174

Earl Pomeroy
Department of History
University of California, San Diego
La Jolla, California 92093

William Stafford
1050 Sunningdale
Lake Oswego, Oregon 97034

Wallace Stegner
13456 South Fork Lane
Los Altos Hills, California 94022

Andrew Suknaski
Writer-in-Residence
Department of English
University of Manitoba
Winnipeg, Manitoba
R3T 1E0

Rosemary Sullivan
Department of English
Erindale College
Mississauga, Ontario
L5L 1C6

Lewis G. Thomas
Department of History
University of Alberta
Edmonton, Alberta
T6G 2E1

Don D. Walker
Department of English
University of Utah
Salt Lake City, Utah 84112

Frank Waters
5630 N. Blue Bonnet Road
Tucson, Arizona 85704

Max Westbrook
Department of English
University of Texas
Austin, Texas 78712

Rudy Wiebe
Department of English
University of Alberta
Edmonton, Alberta
T6G 2E1

Keith Wilson
Department of English
New Mexico State University
Las Cruces, New Mexico 88003

Delbert E. Wylder, Chairman
Department of English
Murray State University
Murray, Kentucky 42071